# REVOLUTION AND CIVIL WAR IN DUBLIN
## 1918–1923
### AN ILLUSTRATED HISTORY

Dublin was the theatre for some of the most iconic events of the Irish revolution. But while images of the Easter Rising have become familiar, the same cannot be said of what came after. Using contemporary documents and images, some of which have never been published before, John Gibney explores the second half of the Irish revolution in Ireland's capital. Beginning in the pivotal year of 1918, he chronicles events such as the conscription crisis, the First World War, the Spanish Flu pandemic, Home Rule, the first Dáil, the War of Independence, the Truce, the Treaty debates and the Civil War. This book opens a unique window into the realities of life in Ireland's capital city from the end of the First World War to the aftermath of the Irish Civil War.

**JOHN GIBNEY,** from Dublin, is currently DFAT 100 Project Coordinator with the Royal Irish Academy's Documents on Irish Foreign Policy project. He has lectured at Trinity College Dublin and University College Dublin and has been a research fellow at the University of Notre Dame and NUI Galway. He worked on the Historical Walking Tours of Dublin until 2015 and is the author of *Dublin: An Illustrated History* (2017), *A Short History of Ireland, 1500–2000* (Yale University Press, 2018) and co-author with Donal Fallon of *Revolutionary Dublin 1912–1923: A Walking Guide* (2018).

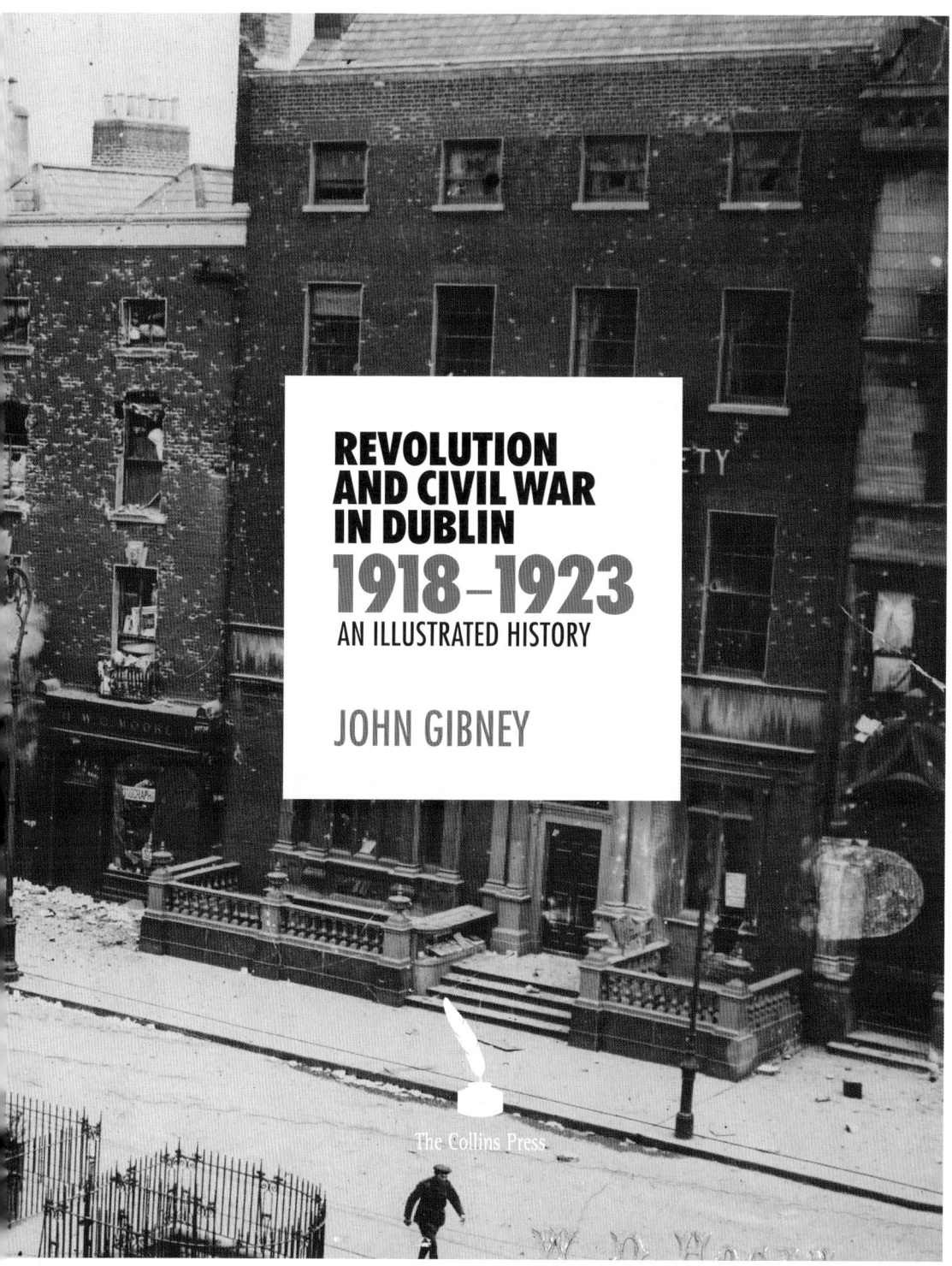

# REVOLUTION AND CIVIL WAR IN DUBLIN

## 1918–1923

### AN ILLUSTRATED HISTORY

JOHN GIBNEY

The Collins Press

# CONTENTS

## ACKNOWLEDGMENTS

I would like to thank the following individuals for helping me to find and reproduce the images held in their care and in their possession: Mairéad Delaney (Abbey Theatre); Conor Dodd and George McCullough (Glasnevin Trust); Mary Feehan; Las Fallon; Lisa Dolan and Noelle Grothier (Military Archives); Máire Kennedy (formerly Dublin City Library and Archive); Berni Metcalfe (National Library of Ireland); Mark Reynolds (GAA Museum); and Aoife Torpey (Kilmainham Gaol Museum). Thanks above all to my family for their love and support. Naturally, any mistakes are my own.

# INTRODUCTION

Dublin was one of the cockpits of the Irish revolution. Ireland's capital city was not, in the early years of the twentieth century, as wealthy or as large as many of its peers. But it was a city of nearly 500,000 people, largely confined within the boundaries of the Royal Canal to the north and the Grand Canal to the south. Unlike many of its counterparts, it was not a city defined by heavy industry, but rather by commerce, trade and administration. Its streetscape had been shaped in the Georgian and Victorian eras, and what was assumed to have been an inexorable decline in its political and social status had ensured that it was a city defined, for both inhabitants and observers, by extremes of wealth and poverty. And between 1912 and 1923 it was also defined as the venue for many of the iconic events of the Irish revolution: the 1913 Lockout, the Easter Rising, the War of Independence and the Civil War.

Why begin any account of the Irish revolution in 1918? While not the most immediately obvious of dates in Ireland's revolutionary period, 1918 remains a crucially important year nonetheless. It was the final year of the First World War, and the political revolution in nationalist Ireland that took place in the aftermath of the Easter Rising of 1916 was accelerated in April 1918 by the prospect of conscription being imposed on Ireland. This shift was registered later it the year, in December, when a newly expanded electorate (which, for the first time, included women) opted for the separatist republicanism of the newly reorganised Sinn Féin over the traditional nationalist demand for Home Rule. The extension of the franchise, the conscription crisis, the end of the 'Great War', the devastating onset of the Spanish Flu pandemic and the general election of December 1918: all were milestones. Following on from this came the struggle for independence in earnest. The meeting of the first Dáil Éireann took place in Dublin's Mansion House (the venue for so many gatherings in these years) in January 1919, but the military conflict spearheaded by the paramilitary Irish Republican Army (IRA) began to gather pace in 1920, as did the British response. From the point of view of Sinn Féin and the IRA, Dublin was a key theatre of conflict: to maintain a foothold in Dublin, and to challenge British power on the streets of Ireland's capital city, was deemed essential by an independence movement that sought to broadcast its credentials internationally in an attempt to secure recognition of an independent Irish state, or to ensure that pressure might be placed upon the British that they might eventually concede such a thing. Dublin was also, especially from late 1920, the stage for some of the most well-known and dramatic events of the War of Independence as a whole: the execution of Kevin Barry, Bloody Sunday and the burning of the Custom House. After the independence movement split over the terms of the Anglo-Irish Treaty of December 1921 that led to the creation the Irish Free State, Dublin became the venue for the opening salvos of the Civil War in June 1922, and much of the 'dirty war' that followed, until the end of the Civil War in April 1923 marked the end of the revolutionary period as a whole

The images assembled here cover many of these events, with the struggle for independence and its aftermath being a key theme. Military conflict acted as a magnet for commercial photographers such as W.D. Hogan (who enjoyed close relations with Sinn Féin and the Free State authorities, and whose collection, much of which is now retained in the National Library of Ireland, features here). Photographers were inevitably drawn to the dramatic. In that sense, the visual record can be skewed. Yet private images and ephemeral publications also illuminate other aspects of life in Dublin in the pages that follow: poverty, wealth, charity, leisure, sport, entertainment, public health, women's rights and the struggles of the labour movement existed alongside the narratives of politics and military action; and often, these may have been more important than either of the latter in the lives of the ordinary and long-departed Dubliners and visitors to Dublin who populate so many of the images. What this book is intended to do is to present a variety of contemporary documents and images in order to open a window onto the second half of the Irish revolution, as experienced in Ireland's capital city.

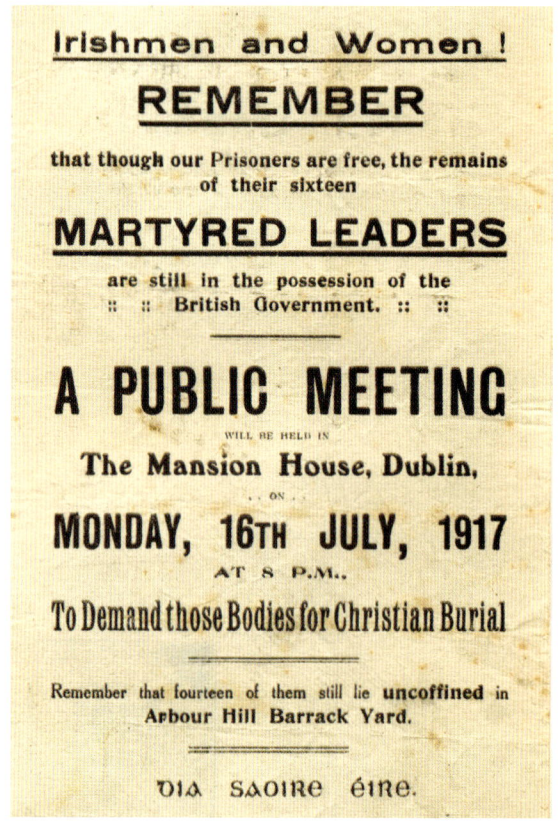

■  Separatist republicanism existed in Ireland prior to 1916 but the Easter Rising of that year was the catalyst that brought it into Ireland's political mainstream. Meetings such as this, held in Dublin's Mansion House – the lord mayor's residence that would feature prominently in events over the years that followed – served to foster and mobilise support for the separatist agenda, turning a military defeat into a political victory in the process (*Dublin City Library and Archive, Birth of the Republic collection*).

■ Dublin in 1895. The city of the late Victorian era was essentially the city of the revolution, as major urban expansion and redevelopment would not take place until after independence. That said, events such as the Easter Rising and the Civil War did significant damage to the city *(New York Public Library)*.

■ Members of Na Fianna Éireann, the republican youth organisation, stand guard around the body of Thomas Ashe in Dublin City Hall, September 1917. Originally from Kerry, Ashe was a teacher and cultural activist who led the most successful action of the Easter Rising outside Dublin when members of the Irish Volunteers under his command defeated a substantial Royal Irish Constabulary (RIC) force at Ashbourne, County Meath, after a five-hour gun battle. Ashe died on 25 September 1917 after being force-fed while on hunger strike in Mountjoy Prison. The circumstances of his death had a powerful resonance in the context of the shifting currents of Irish political life in the wake of the Easter Rising; his funeral in Dublin's Glasnevin Cemetery on 30 September 1917 was an enormous public event that gave republicans in Dublin a focal point around which to mobilise in late 1917 *(Kilmainham Gaol Museum)*.

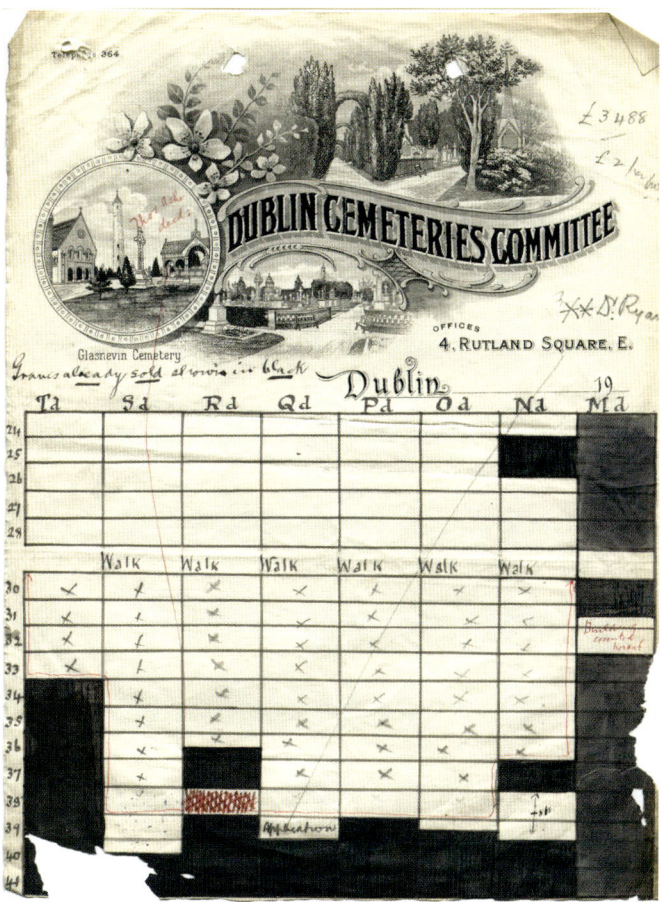

■ A contemporary depiction of graves available in the area of Glasnevin Cemetery now known as the 'republican plot'. Glasnevin had long been a venue for elaborate nationalist and republican funerals, and in the aftermath of the Easter Rising, the idea of a dedicated memorial plot for republicans in the cemetery gathered momentum, and the secretive Irish Republican Brotherhood (IRB) began to purchase the graves that eventually became the republican plot. The starting point was to be the plots clustered around the graves of the IRB leaders James Stephens, John O'Leary, and especially Jeremiah O'Donovan Rossa, whose funeral in August 1915 had been a major public milestone in the prelude to the Easter Rising. The plots that were to be purchased all lay within yards of the enormous tomb of the nineteenth-century nationalist leader Daniel O'Connell. On this document, the rectangular outlines indicate the individual grave plots. The grave highlighted in red is that of Ashe, who at the time of his death was the head of the IRB, and who was buried adjacent to O'Donovan Rossa (Glasnevin Trust).

To the Irish mind for more than a thousand years freedom has had but one definition. It has meant not a limited freedom, a freedom conditioned by the interests of another nation, a freedom compatible with the suzerain authority of a foreign Parliament, but absolute freedom, the sovereign control of Irish destinies. It has meant not the freedom of a class, but the freedom of a people. It has meant not the freedom of a geographical fragment of Ireland, but the freedom of all Ireland, of every sod of Ireland.—**P. H. Pearse.**

Cumann Ʒaeḃealaċ an Ċróic
(CROKE GAELIC CLUB)

# CláR

# CuIRM Ceóil

# náIsIúnta

oiḋċe ḋé luain, ᵹeaḃra 25aḋ, '18

1 ḋtiᵹ an áirḋ ṁaoir

Aɼ a h-Oċt a Clóᵹ.

luaċ                                              pinᵹinn.

Printed by PATRICK MAHON, Yarnhall Street, Dublin.

A flyer for the Croke Gaelic Club (the precise location is unclear). Cultural nationalism remained prominent in Dublin in a period of intensifying political upheaval, though the quotation from Patrick Pearse hints at the political alignment of the club *(Dublin City Library and Archive, Birth of the Republic Collection)*.

A 1918 calendar for the Irish National Foresters, a broadly nationalist benevolent society founded in 1877 (and mercilessly lampooned in Sean O'Casey's play *The Plough and the Stars* (1926), in the form of the sentimental and ineffectual Uncle Peter). The iconography of the calendar is very much that of mainstream Irish nationalism in this era. The Foresters remained active well into the twentieth century *(Kilmainham Gaol Museum)*.

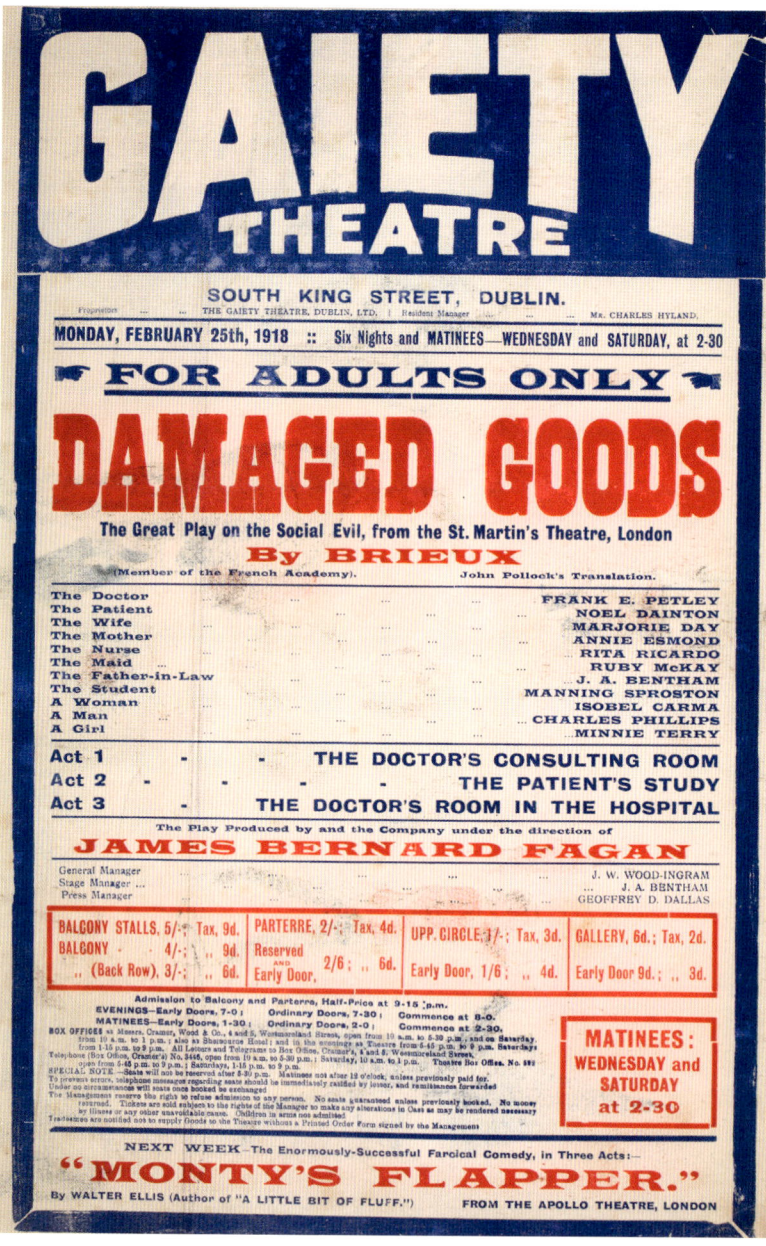

■ Two posters from the Gaiety Theatre in February/March 1918. The first is for *Damaged Goods*, an adaptation of a French play by Eugene Brieux that contained depictions of syphilis, as contracted by one of the characters; hence the 'adults only' notice. The second poster is for D.W. Griffith's epic *Intolerance* (1916), which ranged in scope from ancient Babylon to the modern United States. Griffith was

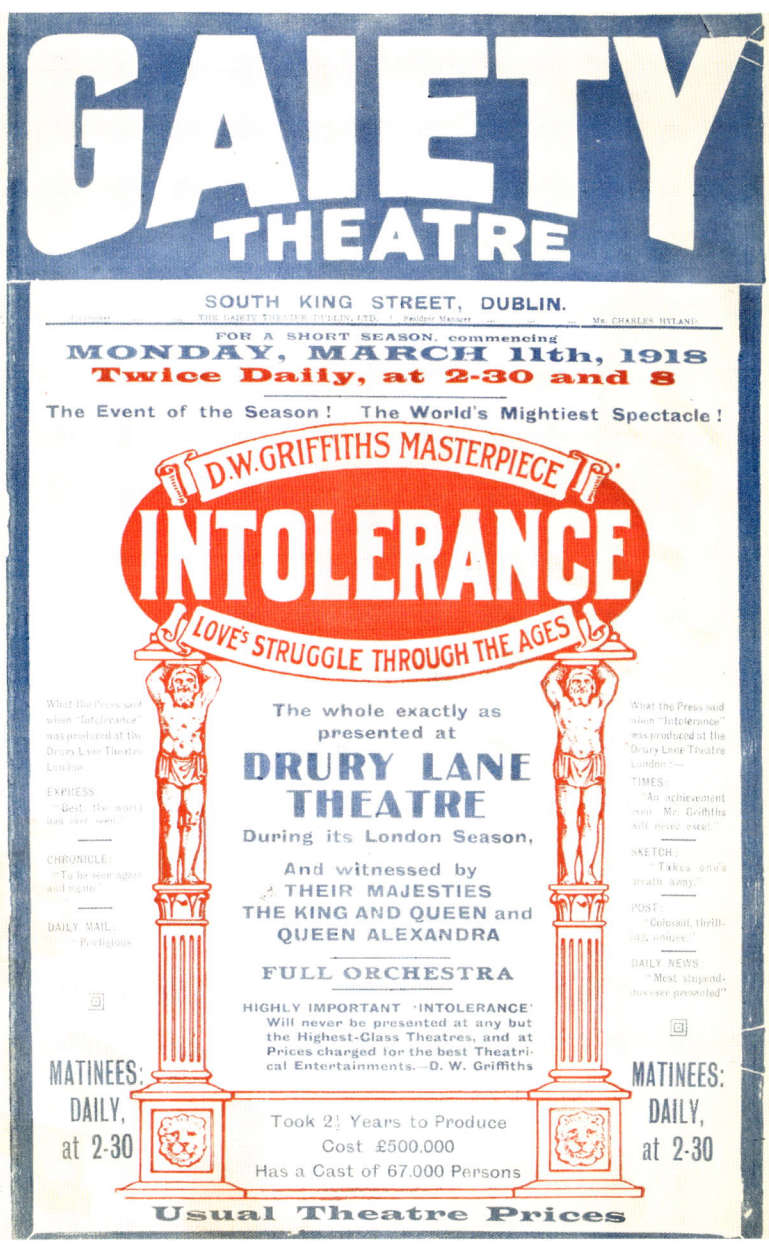

one of the most prominent directors of this era, best known for *The Birth of a Nation*, which was widely condemned for perpetuating racial stereotypes and glorifying the Ku Klux Klan (*Intolerance* was apparently made as a response). Both posters serve as indications of wider cultural influences and leisure activities in the Dublin of 1918 *(National Library of Ireland)*.

The Irish Convention 191.
In full session at Trinity College, Dub

A contemporary sketch of the 'Irish Convention' meeting in Trinity College Dublin's Regent House. The convention was organised by the British government in July 1917 to explore the possibility of finding sufficient consensus between nationalists and unionists to permit the passage of Home Rule in the aftermath of the Easter Rising. It was boycotted by Ulster unionists and Sinn Féin and ultimately proved ineffectual; it met for the last time on 5 April 1918 (*National Library of Ireland*).

# IRELAND & CONSCRIPTION

## UNANIMOUS DECLARATION OF THE MANSION HOUSE CONFERENCE

Thursday, 18th April, 1918. Presided over by the Right Hon. the Lord Mayor of Dublin.

PRESENT: Eamonn de Valera, Arthur Griffith, John Dillon, M.P., Joseph Devlin, M.P., William O'Brien, M.P., T. M. Healy, M.P., W. O'Brien, President Irish Trades Union Congress, Thomas Johnson (Belfast), M. Egan, J.P., T.C. (Cork.)

"TAKING our stand on Ireland's separate and distinct nationhood, and affirming the principle of liberty, that the Governments of nations derive their just powers from the consent of the governed, we deny the right of the British Government or any external authority to impose compulsory military service in Ireland against the clearly expressed will of the Irish people.

"The passing of the Conscription Bill by the British House of Commons must be regarded as a declaration of war on the Irish nation. The alternative to accepting it as such is to surrender our liberties and to acknowledge ourselves slaves. It is in direct violation of the rights of small nationalities to self-determination, which even the Prime Minister of England—now preparing to employ naked militarism and force his Act upon Ireland —himself officially announced as an essential condition for peace at the Peace Congress.

"The attempt to enforce it will be an unwarrantable aggression, which we call upon all Irishmen to resist by the most effective means at their disposal."

### This Declaration was signed by all the Members of the Conference.

Eamonn de Valera, John Dillon, M.P., T. M. Healy, M.P., and W. O'Brien were appointed a delegation from the Mansion House Conference to at once confer with the Archbishops and Bishops then assembled at Maynooth College, Co. Kildare. After hearing the deputation and exchanging views, the Prelates came to the following conclusions:—

The Bishops direct the clergy to celebrate a public Mass of intercession on next Sunday in every church in Ireland to avert the scourge of conscription with which Ireland is now threatened. They further direct that an announcement be made at every public Mass on Sunday next of a public meeting to be held on that day at an hour and place to be specified in the announcement, for the purpose of administering the following pledge against compulsory conscription in Ireland:—

"Denying the right of the British Government to enforce compulsory service in this country, we pledge ourselves solemnly to one another to resist conscription by the most effective means at our disposal."

The clergy are also requested by the Bishops to announce on Sunday next (21st April) that a collection will be held at an early suitable date outside the church gates for the purpose of supplying means to resist the imposition of compulsory military service.

#### THE HIERARCHY'S PRONOUNCEMENT.

An attempt is being made to force conscription upon Ireland against the will of the Irish nation and in defiance of the protests of its leaders.

In view especially of the historic relations between the two countries from the very beginning up to the present moment, we consider that conscription forced in this way upon Ireland is an oppressive and inhuman law, which the Irish people have a right to resist by all the means that are consonant with the law of God.

We wish to remind our people that there is a higher Power which controls the affairs of men. They have in their hands the means of conciliating that Power by strict adherence to the Divine law, by more earnest attention to their religious duties, and by fervent and persevering prayer.

In order to secure the aid of the Holy Mother of God, who shielded our people in the days of their greatest trials, we have already sanctioned a National Novena in honour of Our Lady of Lourdes, commencing on the 3rd May, to secure general and domestic peace.

We also exhort the heads of families to have the Rosary recited every evening with the intention of protecting the spiritual and temporal welfare of our beloved country, and bringing us safe through this crisis of unparalleled gravity.

### The foregoing statement was signed by the following:

✠ His Eminence Cardinal Logue.
✠ Most Rev. Dr. Walsh, Archbishop of Dublin.
✠ Most Rev. Dr. Harty, Archbishop of Cashel.
✠ Most Rev. Dr. Brownrigg, Bishop of Ossory.
✠ Most Rev. Dr. O'Donnell, Bishop of Raphoe.
✠ Most Rev. Dr. Browne, Bishop of Cloyne.
✠ Most Rev. Dr. Hoare, Bishop of Ardagh.
✠ Most Rev. Dr. Foley, Bishop of Kildare and Leighlin.
✠ Most Rev. Dr. Kelly, Bishop of Ross.
✠ Most Rev. Dr. O'Dea, Bishop of Galway.
✠ Most Rev. Dr. Fogarty, Bishop of Killaloe.
✠ Most Rev. Dr. Gaughran, Bishop of Meath.
✠ Most Rev. Dr. M'Hugh, Bishop of Derry.
✠ Most Rev. Dr. M'Kenna, Bishop of Clogher.

✠ Most Rev. Dr. Gilmartin, Bishop of Clonfert.
✠ Most Rev. Dr. Finnegan, Bishop of Kilmore.
✠ Most Rev. Dr. Morrisroe, Bishop of Achonry.
✠ Most Rev. Dr. Naughton, Bishop of Killala.
✠ Most Rev. Dr. Coyne, Bishop of Elphin.
✠ Most Rev. Dr. Cohalan, Bishop of Cork.
✠ Most Rev. Dr. MacRory, Bishop of Down and Connor.
✠ Most Rev. Dr. Hackett, Bishop of Waterford and Lismore.
✠ Most Rev. Dr. Mulhern, Bishop of Dromore.
✠ Most Rev. Dr. O'Sullivan, Bishop of Kerry.
✠ Most Rev. Dr. Codd, Bishop of Ferns.
✠ Most Rev. Dr. Hallinan, Bishop of Limerick.
✠ Most Rev. Dr. Higgins, Bishop of Temno.

Photos by Keogh Bros., Lafayette, Cashman

Wilson, Hartnell & Co., Dublin

The declaration and pledge of the Mansion House conference in opposition to conscription, convened by Laurence O'Neill, the lord mayor of Dublin, on 18 April 1918. In early 1918, German breakthroughs on the Western Front saw the British propose the extension of conscription to Ireland, a move that had been opposed even by the pro-war Irish

Parliamentary Party. In April 1918 it was opposed by all shades of nationalist opinion, the Catholic Church and the labour movement. The pledge was signed nationwide on 21 April 1918 in response to British willingness to impose conscription on Ireland *(Dublin City Library and Archive, Birth of the Republic Collection).*

# IRISH
## Trades Union Congress and Labour Party
### NATIONAL EXECUTIVE, DUBLIN.

# All-Ireland Labour Convention,
## APRIL 20th, 1918, MANSION HOUSE, DUBLIN.

## RESOLUTION.

That this Convention of the Irish Labour movement representing all sections and provinces of Ireland pledge ourselves and those whom we represent that we will not have conscription; that we shall resist it in every way that to us seems feasible; that we claim the right of liberty to decide as units for ourselves, and as a nation for itself; that we place before our brothers in the Labour movement all the world over our claim for independent status as a nation in the International movement, and the right of self-determination as a nation, as to what action or actions our people should take on questions of political or economic issues.

That in view of the great claims on the resources of the National Executive of the Irish Trades Union Congress and Labour Party we hereby call upon the bodies represented here to forward subscriptions for the purpose of enabling them to carry out their campaign against conscription and pledge ourselves to make it a success.

**That this Convention calls upon the workers of Ireland to ABSTAIN FROM WORK on TUESDAY NEXT, APRIL 23rd.**

(1st) As a demonstration of fealty to the cause of Labour and Ireland;

(2nd) As a sign of their resolve to resist the application of the Conscription Act; and

(3rd) For the purpose of enabling every man and woman to sign the pledge of resistance against Conscription.

Believing that our success in resisting the imposition of Conscription will be a signal to the workers of all countries now at war to rise against their oppressors and bring the war to an end, we pledge ourselves in the name of the oppressed of every land in every age to use all means that may be deemed effective to defeat this present conspiracy to enslave our nation.

We call upon all lovers of liberty everywhere to give assistance in this impending struggle.

## THE PLEDGE.

Denying the right of the British Government to enforce compulsory service in this country, we pledge ourselves solemnly to one another to resist Conscription by the most effective means at our disposal.

A poster for an anti-conscription meeting in the Mansion House organised by the labour movement, who held a general strike in protest on 23 April 1918. While Sinn Féin and the IRA understandably attract attention, the labour movement also played a crucial role in the struggle for independence (National Library of Ireland).

# Blacklegs!—made in Dublin

As will be seen from the appended circular letter, attempts are already being set on foot to train women to act as blacklegs in the place of men in the event of Conscription being forced on Ireland. This letter is being circulated through the city.

Let the Chemists' Assistants of Dublin and other parts of Ireland show their disapproval of this man's conduct by dispensing with his assistance in preparing for their examinations.

34 South Frederick Street,

Dublin,

23rd April, 1918.

Dear Sir,

In view of the proposal to apply Conscription to Ireland, which will call up many Pharmaceutical Assistants, I beg to say that I am prepared to train ladies in Prescription Reading, Weighing and Measuring, and the Principles of Dispensing, as rapidly and thoroughly as possible, so as to make them useful Medical Hall Assistants to fill the vacancies.

Your co-operation in making this known, and any suggestions you may make, will be greatly valued.

Yours faithfully,

J. A. RAY, B.A., M.P.S.I.

Concrete measures against conscription: a call to name and shame employers, such as the chemist in question, who might facilitate its imposition *(National Library of Ireland)*.

■ An official proclamation banning public assemblies in Dublin *(National Library of Ireland).*

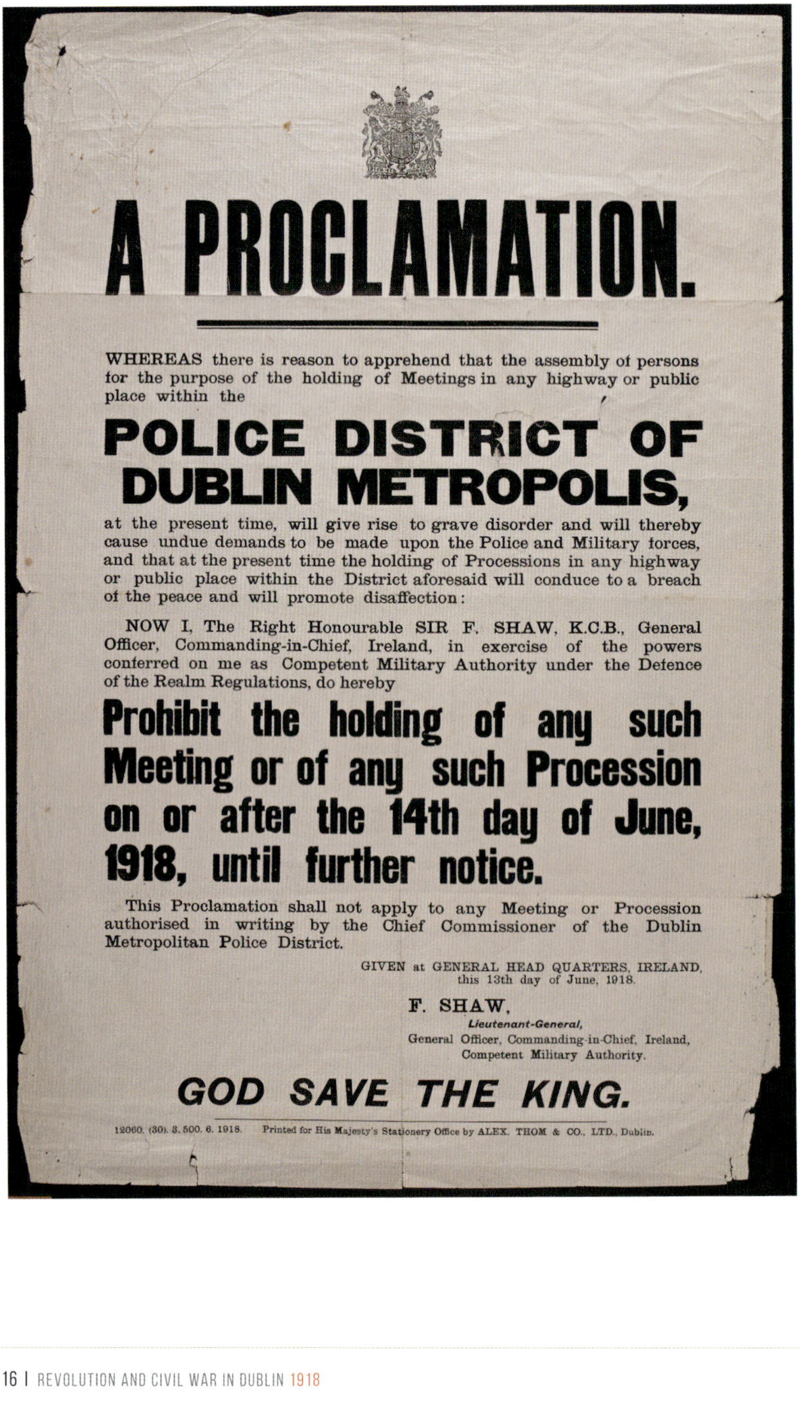

# A PROCLAMATION.

WHEREAS there is reason to apprehend that the assembly of persons for the purpose of the holding of Meetings in any highway or public place within the

## POLICE DISTRICT OF DUBLIN METROPOLIS,

at the present time, will give rise to grave disorder and will thereby cause undue demands to be made upon the Police and Military forces, and that at the present time the holding of Processions in any highway or public place within the District aforesaid will conduce to a breach of the peace and will promote disaffection:

NOW I, The Right Honourable SIR F. SHAW, K.C.B., General Officer, Commanding-in-Chief, Ireland, in exercise of the powers conferred on me as Competent Military Authority under the Defence of the Realm Regulations, do hereby

## Prohibit the holding of any such Meeting or of any such Procession on or after the 14th day of June, 1918, until further notice.

This Proclamation shall not apply to any Meeting or Procession authorised in writing by the Chief Commissioner of the Dublin Metropolitan Police District.

GIVEN at GENERAL HEAD QUARTERS, IRELAND,
this 13th day of June, 1918.

**F. SHAW,**
*Lieutenant-General,*
General Officer, Commanding-in-Chief, Ireland,
Competent Military Authority.

## GOD SAVE THE KING.

12060. (30). 3. 500. 6. 1918.     Printed for His Majesty's Stationery Office by ALEX. THOM & CO., LTD., Dublin.

The 1918 Ard Fheis of Na Fianna Éireann, the republican boy scout movement originally founded in 1909, held at the Mansion House. Members of Na Fianna had fought in the Easter Rising, and the organisation was often a stepping stone towards involvement in the Irish Volunteers and Irish Republican Army (IRA). Note the Fianna flag *(National Library of Ireland).*

■ This advertisement for wartime outfits for women shows the extent to which the First World War penetrated all levels of popular culture in Ireland *(Dublin City Library and Archive).*

The Phoenix Park, as photographed by the Royal Air Force on 21 August 1918. The Viceregal Lodge (now Áras an Uachtaráin) is visible at the bottom right of the picture. In the top right a series of jagged outlines can be seen between the clusters of trees above the road (Chesterfield Avenue); these are training trenches dug during the First World War to prepare troops for theatres of war such as the Western Front. The Phoenix Park was originally laid out in the 1670s and had long been a venue for military activities; this continued during the First World War *(Conor Dodd)*.

Documents relating to the sinking of the RMS *Leinster*, which was torpedoed by a U-boat just outside Dublin Bay on 10 October after leaving Kingstown (Dún Laoghaire) harbour, with the loss of over 580 lives. One of the survivors was the eighteen-year-old Private Victor B. Rummings, stationed in Limerick with the Scottish Horse and who, on 8 October 1918, went on leave and left Limerick, using the railway ticket (page 22), to visit his family in Bath. He was a passenger on the *Leinster*; as shown by the two telegrams to his mother (facing page), he was initially feared lost but was rescued and brought back to Dublin. Many of the military personnel killed on the *Leinster* were later buried in Grangegorman Military Cemetery, while civilian dead were interred in cemeteries such as Glasnevin. The photograph below shows some of the military survivors in Dublin *(Conor Dodd)*.

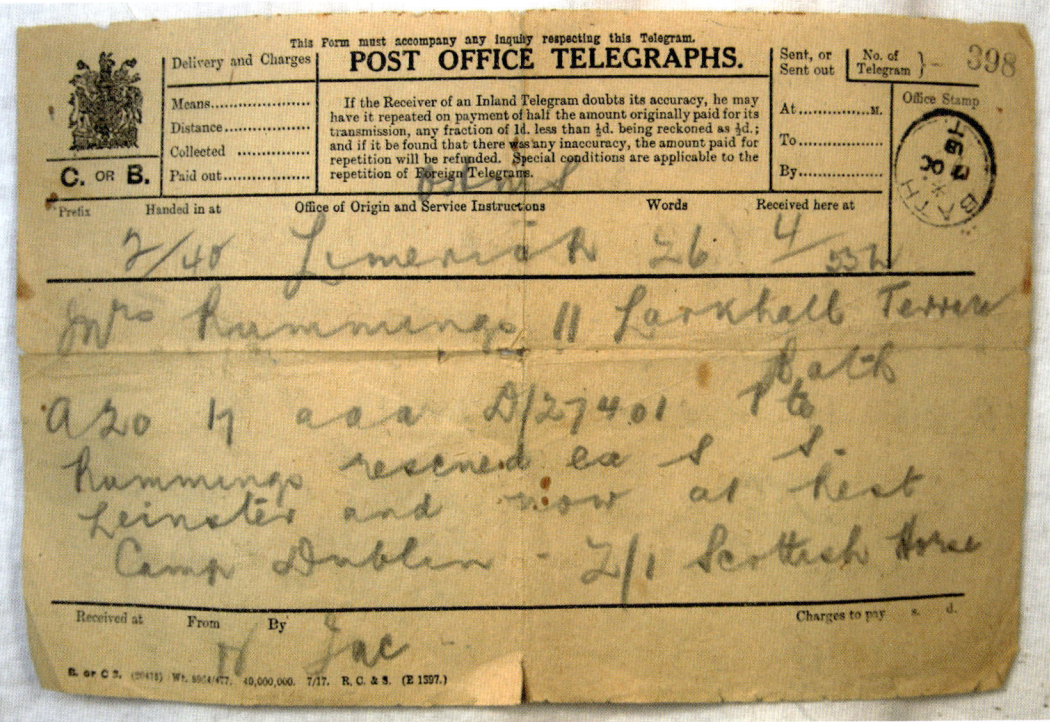

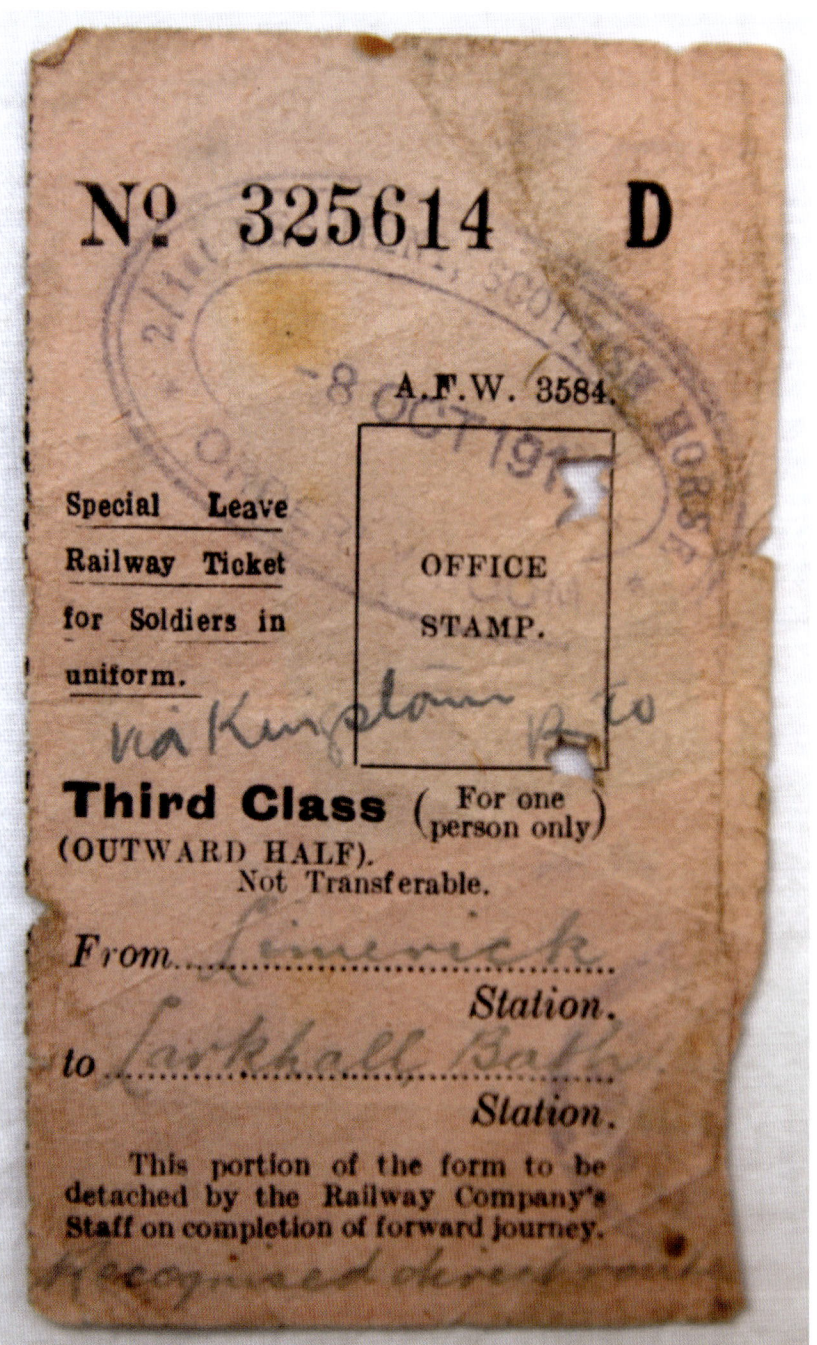

Dublin city centre from the air, looking towards the mouth of the River Liffey, as photographed by the Royal Air Force on 5 November 1918 *(Conor Dodd)*.

■ Pages from the burial register for Prospect (Glasnevin) Cemetery for 3–4 November 1918, in which over half of those buried were recorded as having died from influenza. The Spanish Flu pandemic of 1918–19 may have killed as many as 100 million people as it swept across the globe. It killed at least 20,000 in Ireland; over 2,800 deaths were officially attributed to flu in Dublin city and county. The death toll from related illnesses was almost certainly much higher because the disease spread rapidly in the cramped conditions of the inner city *(Glasnevin Trust)*.

**Russian Revolution & Republic Committee**
(DUBLIN TRADES COUNCIL & CUMANNACHT NA hEIREANN)

**FIRST ::
ANNUAL COMMEMORATION**
(Cuimnin Cinn bliaḋna)
OF THE
(ar)

# Russian Revolution
(an éirġe amaċ 'ran Rúir)
AND THE
(aġus ar)

# Soviet Republic
(Poblaċt an luċt oibre)
IN THE

# MANSION HOUSE

## Monday, 18th November
AT 8 P.M.

" Are France, Italy, Great Britain and the United States willing to recognise the right to Self-Determination of their own destinies in the case of the Peoples of **IRELAND**, Egypt, India, Madagasar, Indo-China, and other Countries? To refuse this right to these Peoples would mean the putting forward of the programme of the most synical Imperialism."—Trotsky, Dec. 29, 1917

**Long Live the Workers' Republic !
Long Live the Soviet of Free Russia !
Long Live the International !**

A poster for a meeting on 18 November in the Mansion House to commemorate the Russian revolution, a reminder that Ireland's revolution took place against the backdrop of global upheaval *(National Library of Ireland)*.

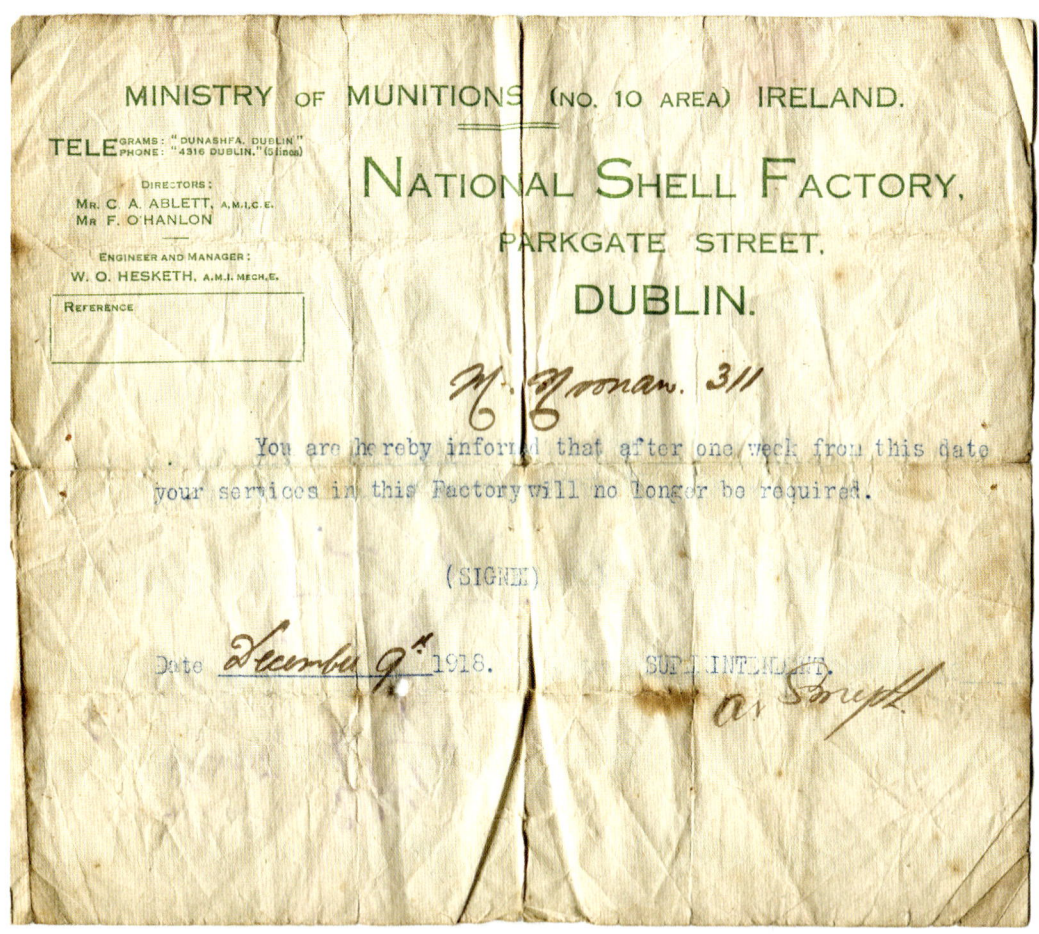

MINISTRY OF MUNITIONS (NO. 10 AREA) IRELAND.

TELE GRAMS: "DUNASHFA, DUBLIN"
PHONE: "4316 DUBLIN." (5 lines)

## NATIONAL SHELL FACTORY,

DIRECTORS:
MR C. A. ABLETT, A.M.I.C.E.
MR F. O'HANLON

### PARKGATE STREET,

ENGINEER AND MANAGER:
W. O. HESKETH, A.M.I. MECH.E.

# DUBLIN.

REFERENCE

*M Noonan. 311*

You are hereby informed that after one week from this date your services in this Factory will no longer be required.

(SIGNED)

Date *December 9th* 1918.        SUPERINTENDENT

■ A note to one May Noonan, a worker in the National Shell Factory in Parkgate Street, advising that she would be let go as the factory ceased production following the end of the First World War. Such 'war industries', manufacturing munitions and other military material, existed in Ireland during the war, though never on the scale of their British counterparts (Conor Dodd).

Female workers in the National Shell Factory. Just as in the rest of the UK, war industries brought Irishwomen into the workforce in unprecedented numbers. May Noonan is second from left in the back row *(Conor Dodd)*.

■ Richard Coleman. Originally from Swords, in north County Dublin, Coleman had led the local company of the Irish Volunteers in the town and was a close associate of Thomas Ashe. During the Easter Rising he had mobilised under Ashe and also saw action at the Mendicity Institution in Dublin. He was imprisoned in Dartmoor after the Rising and was imprisoned again in Usk, in Wales, as part of the 'German Plot' arrests of 1918, in which large numbers of republicans were detained on spurious charges of conspiring with the Germans. He subsequently died of pneumonia during the influenza pandemic. Like that of Ashe, his funeral in Glasnevin Cemetery on 9 December 1918 was a major show of strength by republicans *(Military Archives)*.

Members of Sinn Féin at the somewhat dilapidated rear of the party's headquarters at no. 6 Harcourt Street in Dublin. This was formerly the home of Cardinal John Henry Newman, the first rector of the Catholic University of Ireland in the 1850s, which was one of the institutions that later evolved into University College Dublin. Some senior figures in the independence movement are visible: Michael Collins is fourth from left in the second row, with Desmond Fitzgerald sixth from the left in the same row *(Mercier Archives)*.

■ A Sinn Féin poster anticipating the 1918 general election, clearly showing how the prospect of the recognition of Irish independence by the post-war peace conference was a key element in Sinn Féin's political platform *(Dublin City Library and Archive, Birth of the Republic Collection)*.

## SINN FEIN.

### TO EACH ELECTOR OF THE

# Stephen's Green Division

A General Election is expected before the end of this year. Sinn Fein means, through it, to let the world know the **REAL NATURE OF IRELAND'S DEMAND.**

All the belligerents in the world war claim to stand for the principle of **THE FREEDOM OF NATIONALITIES, GREAT AND SMALL.** That principle will be the **TEST OF THEIR SINCERITY WHEN PEACE IS DISCUSSED.**

The enemies of Ireland are trying, and will try, to represent the Irish Claim, not as **A NATIONAL CLAIM FOR INDEPENDENCE, BUT** as a **DOMESTIC PROBLEM WITHIN THE BRITISH EMPIRE.**

These enemies will point to the participation of Irish representatives in Westminster politics as a proof that the question is a domestic one.

**SINN FEIN IS GOING TO REMOVE THAT ARGUMENT AT THE COMING ELECTION** by giving Nationalists in every constituency, yours included, an opportunity **TO CAST THEIR VOTES FOR NATIONAL INDEPENDENCE, AND NOTHING LESS.**

In order to gain this great object it asks your help. **ELECTIONS ARE EXPENSIVE,** but if every Nationalist vote be not cast for Independence we lose **THE GREATEST CHANCE OF CENTURIES FOR WINNING IRISH FREEDOM.**

Therefore we appeal to you, when you are asked by **SINN FEIN** Collectors (who will, if required, produce their authority), to subscribe towards the cost of **FIGHTING THE ELECTION IN STEPHEN'S GREEN DIVISION** as generously as your means will permit, and thus, as well as by your vote and influence, to enable **SINN FEIN**

**TO PUT YOUR COUNTRY'S REAL CASE BEFORE THE WORLD.**

An election leaflet for Sinn Féin candidate and veteran Dublin city alderman Thomas Kelly from the December 1918 general election *(National Library of Ireland)*.

A flyer from the 1918 general election, fought on the newly extended franchise, for the Stephen's Green ward, clearly showing how the war was an issue in the election. Thomas Kelly won the seat for Sinn Féin by a huge majority, defeating the unionist candidate, the barrister and journalist Henry Hanna *(National Library of Ireland)*.

What **HANNA** has done for the Irish Soldiers :—

For Four Years

He has collected **FUNDS** for Prisoners of War, and Comforts for Men of

## IRISH REGIMENTS.

He has worked for the Wounded and Disabled as Secretary of Irish Counties War Hospital, Glasnevin.

He has helped to raise and administer over £37,000 for Irish Soldiers.

What **BRADY** has done for the Irish Soldiers

**? ? ?**

What **KELLY** has done for the Irish Soldiers

**? ? ?**

Printed and Published by George F. Healy & Co., Ltd., 23 Lower Ormond Quay, Dublin, for the Election Agent, S. H Crawford, Solicitor, Foster Place, Dublin.

GREAT ~~Art.~~ 3 DEC 1918

**ctory CONCERT**

Commandant Eamonn De Valera
M.I.P.

**:: New Year's Eve ::
Mansion House, Dublin**

1918

An advertisement for the victory concert to mark Sinn Féin's stunning performance in the post-war general election, in which they won 73 out of 105 Irish parliamentary seats; Éamon de Valera, the party leader, features prominently. Born in New York but raised in Clare, de Valera had commanded a company of the Irish Volunteers in Dublin during the Easter Rising; after the death of Thomas Ashe, he was the most senior survivor of the rising and in September 1917 had become leader of Sinn Féin as it was reorganised into an explicitly separatist party *(Dublin City Library and Archive, Birth of the Republic Collection).*

# 1919

An official poster depicting the first meeting of Dáil Eireann. Sinn Féin had run its electoral candidates on an abstentionist ticket, pledging not to take their seats in Westminster if elected. Sinn Féin's new parliamentarians who were not imprisoned or on the run met in the Round Room of the Mansion House on 21 January 1919 (the same day as the Soloheadbeg ambush in Tipperary, which is usually taken as marking the start of the War of Independence). Ironically, the Mansion House had hosted a reception for veterans of the Royal Dublin Fusiliers (the principal British unit that recruited from Dublin) earlier that afternoon. At the first meeting of the Dáil, a 'Democratic Programme' was read, which declared that 'we desire our country to be ruled in accordance with the principles of Liberty, Equality, and Justice for all, which alone can secure permanence of Government in the willing adhesion of the people'. The Dáil was viewed as an illegitimate assembly by the London government, and was thus declared illegal in April 1919 *(National Library of Ireland).*

A government proclamation announcing the further easing of the restrictions on businesses that had been imposed under the wartime Defence of the Realm Act. To give but one example, here retail shops are permitted to open until 9.30 p.m., whereas in the equivalent regulations that had been issued on 11 November (and which are referred to here), they had been obliged to close at 5.30 p.m., an indication that life was returning to something resembling pre-war normality as the First World War had come to an end *(National Library of Ireland)*.

# EARLY CLOSING ORDER.

## By the Lords Justices-General and General Governors of Ireland.

### JAMES H. CAMPBELL.

WHEREAS by Order dated the 11th day of November, 1918, duly made under the Defence of the Realm Regulations, provision was made for restricting, during the period and subject to the terms, conditions and exceptions in the said Order expressed and mentioned, the hours in the evening during which trade or business may be carried on:

And whereas the said Order was varied and amended by further Orders dated respectively the 16th day of November, 1918, the 14th day of December, 1918, and the 1st day of February, 1919:

And whereas it appears to Us expedient that certain clauses of the said Orders should be revoked, and that the said Orders should be further varied and amended in manner hereinafter appearing:

Now in pursuance of Regulation 10B of the Defence of the Realm Regulations, We, the Lords Justices-General and General Governors of Ireland, hereby order and declare as follows:—

I. That from and after the date of this Order for clauses 2, 3, 4, 7 and 10 of the said Order of the 11th day of November, 1918, the following clauses shall be substituted:—

(2) Every retail shop, including premises licensed for the sale of intoxicating liquor on or off the premises, in the County Boroughs of Dublin, Belfast, Cork, Limerick, Londonderry and Waterford, and every office connected therewith (save as hereinafter provided) shall be closed for the serving of customers not later than 9.30 o'clock, p.m., on every week-day;

Provided that—

Shops carrying on the business of the sale of hot fish or shell fish cooked on the premises may remain open up to but not later than 10.30 o'clock, p.m.:

(3) No meals shall be cooked after the hour of 9.30 o'clock, p.m., in any Licensed Hotel, Restaurant, or Railway Refreshment Rooms:

(4) Every Retail Shop not being in one of the said County Boroughs and every office connected therewith (save as hereinafter provided) shall be closed for the serving of customers not later than 9.30 o'clock, p.m., on every week-day.

Provided that—

Licensed Hotels, Restaurants, and Railway Refreshment Rooms may be kept open for the service of meals after the hour of 9.30 o'clock, p.m., but not for the sale or service of intoxicating liquors:

(7) Theatres, Pictures Houses, and other places of entertainment conducted for profit and open to the public during the day shall in no case remain open to a later hour than 10.30 o'clock, p.m., on every week-day, provided that this Regulation shall not apply in any case in which special permission shall be obtained from the Representative in Ireland of the Coal Controller to hold any performance which would otherwise contravene this Regulation; and the Representative in Ireland of the Coal Controller may give such permission on such terms as may seem to him proper:

(10) Banks (other than Savings Banks) shall not be open to the public for the transaction of business to a later hour than 3 o'clock, p.m.:

II. From and after the date of this Order Clause 5 of the said Order of the 11th day of November, 1918, Clauses 2 and 3 of the said Order of the 14th day of December, 1918, and the whole of the said Order of the 1st day of February, 1919, shall be revoked:

III. This Order shall be read and construed with the said Orders of the 11th day of November, 1918, the 16th day of November, 1918, and the 14th day of December, 1918.

Given at His Majesty's Castle of Dublin, this 28th day of February, 1919.

By Their Excellencies' Command,

### J. J. TAYLOR.

12636. (66) 3. 8,500. 3. 1919.   Printed for His Majesty's Stationery Office by A. THOM & CO., Ltd., Dublin.

# MANSION HOUSE, DUBLIN.

# A PROCLAMATION!

**Whereas** it has come to my knowledge that "The Competent Military Authorities" fear that the reception to be given to Mr. DE VALERA on Wednesday evening, on his return to this country after having been interned in an English Jail for close on 10 months without any charge or without any trial "will give rise to grave disorder and will thereby cause undue demands to be made upon the Police and the Military Forces":

**And Whereas** I am the one charged more directly with the peace and order of this City, I dissent wholly from the view that grave disorder is impending, but having as Chief Magistrate done not a little to keep the peace and good order of this City for the past two years, I now therefore respectfully request my fellow-citizens, in my capacity as Lord Mayor and charged with the responsibilities of that Office, to follow my advice and give no opportunity for provocative action, which might cloud the prospects of the Nation during the Peace Conference.

## LAURENCE O'NEILL,

25th MARCH, 1919.

*Lord Mayor of Dublin.*

# God Save Ireland!

DOLLARD, Printinghouse, Dublin, Ltd.

A proclamation issued by the Lord Mayor of Dublin, Laurence O'Neill, in defiance of British attempts to restrict the welcoming ceremony for Éamon de Valera, who, with the assistance of Harry Boland and Michael Collins, had recently escaped from Lincoln Gaol. De Valera had been imprisoned there as part of the 'German Plot' arrests of May 1918, based on British allegations that members of Sinn Féin were conspiring with the Germans. O'Neill, who had sat on Dublin Corporation since 1910, was an independent nationalist, sympathetic to separatism but well regarded across Ireland's political spectrum *(National Library of Ireland)*.

Three key figures in the independence movement at the second session of the first Dáil, held in the Mansion House, 1 April 1919. (L–r): Éamon de Valera, Michael Collins and Harry Boland. This was de Valera's first public appearance in Ireland after his escape. All three were prominent in Sinn Féin, were veterans of the Easter Rising and had been imprisoned for their involvement in it. Boland, from Dublin, was a senior figure in both the Irish Republican Brotherhood (IRB) and Gaelic Athletic Association (GAA), Collins was prominent in the IRB and the emergent Irish Republican Army (IRA), while de Valera, as president of Sinn Féin, was the figurehead of the independence movement. The Dáil was declared illegal soon after this photograph was taken and the following June, de Valera embarked on a lengthy publicity and fund-raising tour of the US, accompanied by Boland (National Library of Ireland).

- A circular about the welcome arrangements for Constance Markievicz after her release from prison in March 1919. Markievicz was born into the Anglo-Irish Gore-Booth family of Sligo, and married a Polish count (hence the surname and the usual description of her as 'Countess'). She had become a socialist and was active in the 1913 Lockout and the 1916 Rising, the latter as a member of James Connolly's Irish Citizen Army. She remained active in the independence movement and was incarcerated in the 'German Plot' arrests of 1918. By the time of her release she had the distinction of being the first woman ever elected to Westminster, as MP for St Patrick's in Dublin; in line with party policy she declined to take her seat and instead was appointed Minister for Labour in the Dáil government *(Kilmainham Gaol Museum)*.

## ~ IRISH CITIZEN ARMY. ~

*Headquarters—*

12th March, 1919.

A Chara,

It has been decided to arrange a public reception for The Countess, on Saturday evening next, and we shall be glad if your organisation will attend.

Copy of arrangements enclosed. Please inform your various units.

Should you decide on sending a deputation to meet her at Kingstown, it should not be disappointed at any delay there, as we are making arrangements for her to have some refreshments before coming to Town by motor.

Is mise, do Chara,

J. O'NEILL,

Commandant.

ARRANGEMENTS FOR RECEPTION OF

COUNTESS MARKIEVICZ

All bodies to be in their allotted places by 6.15 p.m.

on Saturday, march 15th, 1919.

1.  I.C.A. and James' Band in Beresford Place.

2.  Fianna. Eden Quay, south side.

3.  Cumann na mBan. Eden Quay, north side,
    Head on Beresford Place.

4.  Inghinidhe na h-Eireann. Eden Quay, north side,
    immediately behind No.3.

5.  Irish Women's Franchise League. Eden Quay, north side,
    immediately behind No.4.

6.  Sinn Fein bodies. Marlborough Street, east side,
    head on Eden Quay.

7.  Trades bodies. Marlborough Street, west side,
    head on Eden Quay.

8.  Irish Volunteers. Eden Quay, north side, and O'Connell
    Street, head on Marlborough Street.

ROUTE:

    Beresford Place, Gardiner Street, Parnell Street,
    O'Connell Street, Westmoreland Street, Dame Street,
    Lord Edward Street, High Street, Corn Market, Francis
    Street, to New Street, where a Meeting will be held.

The Procession will march in the order outlined above.

    - : - : - : - : - : -

More precise details of the welcoming ceremony detailing what organisations
were to assemble in the vicinity of Liberty Hall on Beresford Place, the
headquarters of the Irish Transport and General Workers Union (ITGWU) and
the Irish Labour Party *(Military Archives)*.

Constance Markievicz (centre) pictured in Liberty Hall on the night of her release from prison *(National Library of Ireland)*.

A satirical postcard depicting the escape of twenty republican prisoners from Mountjoy Prison on 29 March 1919 *(Kilmainham Gaol Museum).*

CAPT. H. SYKES. I. W.
N. Dublin Union     April 1919

Portrait photographs of British officers stationed in the North Dublin Union, April 1919. Located near Smithfield, this was originally one of Dublin's two workhouses, but had been taken over by the British Army in July–August 1918; its residents were moved over to the South Dublin Union, near the modern site of St James's Hospital. It was later used to house prisoners by both the British and later the Irish Free State government at the end of the Irish Civil War (Conor Dodd).

HASKINS

N. Dublin Union    April 1919

G. Crichton

N. Dublin Union. Abril 1919

■ Harry Boland in Croke Park, 1919. Boland was a prominent member of the GAA, having played for Dublin in the 1909 All-Ireland hurling final (they lost to Tipperary in a replay, albeit without Boland) and serving in a wide range of administrative roles, including as chairman of the county board from 1913. The association itself was a product of the late Victorian cultural revival in Ireland, and was broadly nationalist. While many of its officials were strongly republican, they generally tried to ensure that the GAA steered a course between the various competing segments of Irish nationalism. It was only after the Easter Rising of 1916 that it became more obviously associated with separatism, though the vast majority of those who fought in the rising were not actually members *(National Library of Ireland).*

A poster for an ITGWU meeting in the Mansion House, June 1922. The ITGWU was founded by James Larkin in 1909 and was best known for its role in the 1913 Lockout. After 1916 it took a more nationalistic line on key issues and also recovered dramatically from the damage it had suffered during the lockout, from having perhaps 5,000 members nationwide in 1916 to over 100,000 by 1919 *(National Library of Ireland)*.

# Irish Transport & General Workers' Union

## SPECIAL GENERAL

# MEETING

### OF DUBLIN MEMBERS

WILL BE HELD IN

## ROUND ROOM, MANSION HOUSE,

— ON —

## Sunday Next, 22nd June, 1919,

### AT 12.30 A.M., SHARP.

*Punctual Attendance urgently requested.*

**A Full Statement with reference to the National Health Insurance Department will be submitted.**

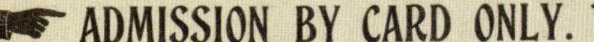 ☞ **ADMISSION BY CARD ONLY.** ☜

**THOMAS FORAN,**
*General President*

A receipt for Clara Doyle's donation to the Dáil loan. In order to raise funds for its activities, the Dáil organised a fund-raising drive under the stewardship of Michael Collins, who was its Minister for Finance. *(Dublin City Library and Archive, Birth of a Republic Collection).*

Detach this part and return to Subscriber.                                          No....6.7....

**GOVERNMENT OF THE IRISH REPUBLIC.**
**5 per cent. Registered Certificates (1919) (Internal).**

Date, *20th September* 1919.

RECEIVED from *Miss Clara Doyle*

of *3 Chancery St. Dublin*

the sum of *one* pounds, *_____* shillings, being the amount payable on application for:—

*1 Certificate of £1 (1.0)*

MICHAEL O COILEAIN, Minister of Finance.

£1 *_____*                    Per *Mary*

Preserve this receipt carefully. It will be exchanged in due course for the definite certificate.

Archbishop William Walsh of Dublin outlines his reasons for supporting the republican fund-raising drive. Known for his concern for Dublin's poor, Walsh had made no public comment on the 1916 Rising, but was sympathetic to separatism, having publicly supported Joe McGuinness, the successful Sinn Féin candidate in the 1917 Longford by-election; his intervention in that contest was assumed to have helped McGuinness *(Dublin City Library and Archive, Birth of a Republic Collection).*

## LETTER FROM HIS GRACE THE MOST REV. DR. WALSH, ARCHBISHOP OF DUBLIN, TO HIS EMINENCE CARDINAL O'CONNELL OF AMERICA

Archbishop's House, Dublin,
10th November, 1919.

My dear Lord Cardinal,

I wish to contribute a hundred uineas (£105 sterling) to the Irish National Fund inaugurated under the auspices of the elected body known as Dail Eireann, our Irish Parliament. I cannot but think that, as far as our people of Irish race are concerned, their knowledge of the fact that I have subscribed to the Fund would be of at least as much help as any money subscription of mine could be.

But as matters now stand in Ireland, none of our newspapers dare publish the fact that I have subscribed. We are living under martial law, and amongst the numerous devices to which our present government has had recourse in its foolish attempts to crush the national spirit of our people is the issuing of sundry military orders. In one of these they have given notice to the editors or managers of our popular newspapers to the effect that the fate of any newspaper venturing to publish the names of contributors to the Fund, or the amounts contributed, will be immediate suppression.

I am, of course, well aware of the deep personal interest that your Eminence takes in our Irish national affairs, and of the powerful help that you have given to our people in their effort to secure their rightful control of the government of their own country. I trust that your Eminence will not consider it a misplaced confidence on my part that I feel assured of your willingness to come to my aid by helping me to make known in America the fact of my subscription to the Dail Eireann Fund.

Freedom of the Press, the right of public meeting, the right of personal liberty, even the right of trial by jury, no longer exist in this country, except so far as they can exist subject to the absolutely uncontrolled discretion of some military ruler technically designated the "competent military authority."

All this has had its natural effect—the driving of disaffection under ground—with the no less natural result that disaffection driven under ground, finds an outlet in crime.

The "competent military authorities" do not seem to realise that there is no possible remedy fo this lamentable state of things so long as the source of all the evil—the present system of military rule in Ireland—is maintained. Apologising for this intrusion, I have the honour to remain, your Eminence's devoted servant in Christ,

✠ WILLIAM J. WALSH.
Archbishop of Dublin.

A ballad commemorating Martin Savage, a 21-year-old IRA member from ▶
Sligo, who was killed in an exchange of gunfire on the Navan Road after the
IRA attempted to ambush the Lord Lieutenant, Sir John French, 1st Viscount
French of Ypres, en route to the Viceregal Lodge in the Phoenix Park on 19
December 1919. The assassination had been planned originally for Armistice
Day, 11 November. He survived, and Savage was the only casualty. Some in
the IRA wanted to use the funeral as a show of strength, but this was deemed
unwise in the changed climate of 1919. Ballads like these were an integral
element of popular culture in this era, and could often be harnessed to political
ends, as was the case here (*National Library of Ireland*).

The Armistice Day parade of 11 November 1919 passes through College Green marking the first anniversary of the ending of the First World War. College Green would remain a major venue for Armistice Day events into the 1920s *(Mercier Archives)*.

# On Ashtown Road,

Martin Savage, I.R.A., Killed in Action
December 19th, 1919.

Air: "Snowy Breasted Pearl."

One cold December Day,
A motor ploughed its way,
Mid bullets flash and play,
    On Ashtown Road.

In that car a living tool,
Of England's hated rule,
And there began a duel
    On Ashtown Road.

Young Savage undismayed,
With bomb and hand grenade,
Attacked them unafraid
    On Ashtown Road.

But a bullet laid him low,
From the rifles of the foe,
Ye another debt we owe
    For Ashtown Road.

Who dies for Ireland lives,
For her their life blood gives,
As this noble lad gave his
    On Ashtown Road·

They laid him in the grave,
Where leafless branches wave,
Oh ! son of Erin brave,
    Farewell to thee.

# Óglaiġ na h-Éireann

### D & E COMPANIES—2ND BATTALION —DUBLIN BRIGADE.

❧

:: SECOND ::

# ANNUAL CEILIDHE

WILL BE HELD IN

## THE BANBA HALL, PARNELL SQUARE,

ON

### SATURDAY, 29th NOVEMBER, 1919.

## TICKETS (Single) 4/- ✢ Dancing at 9.30 p.m.

### PAY AT DOOR.

◼ An advertisement for the 'second annual ceilidhe' for the Dublin Brigade of the Irish Volunteers, who even at this stage were increasingly being known as the IRA. Social events such as these were also intended to raise funds for the organisation, which had been declared 'dangerous' by the British authorities in July 1918, which meant that public assemblies by such bodies were illegal. The use of the Irish name for the Volunteers ('Óglaigh na hÉireann') may have been an attempt to sidestep this restriction, though it is unclear whether or not it took place. The Irish Volunteers, along with Sinn Féin, were banned outright in September 1919 (*National Library of Ireland*).

An RIC sergeant points out a bullet hole in Lord French's car after the IRA ambush. The early activities of the IRA in Dublin consisted of assassinations of policemen and officials; this was a step up. French was born in Kent but had strong family connections to Ireland. He enjoyed a lengthy military career across the British Empire but was criticised for his leadership of the British Expeditionary Force in the early years of the First World War and resigned his commission. Having been appointed Lord Lieutenant of Ireland, part of his brief was to prepare for the implementation of Home Rule but, believing that the suppression of unrest was essential to this, his policies in Ireland were heavy-handed. As he was returning from Ashtown railway station, he was ambushed at Kelly's Corner on the Navan Road on 19 December 1919 by IRA members led by Dan Breen; the car was attacked with grenades but accelerated to safety. *(National Library of Ireland).*

A depiction of a 'peace wedding' in All Saints Church, Blackrock, by Henry Love of Monkstown, first exhibited in 1920 at the Dublin Sketching Club. The flags indicate the loyalties of Dublin's sizeable Protestant community, many members of which had also served in the First World War. Dublin had the largest Protestant population outside north-east Ulster; indeed, the only unionist MP elected outside Ulster in the 1918 election was Sir Maurice Dockrell, who was elected for Rathmines. In political terms, however, the unionist sympathies of Dublin Protestants became redundant after independence; unionism simply did not command enough support in the Irish Free State. That said, proof of a continuing affinity to the British monarchy and Empire was seen in the fact that union flags were commonly displayed in parts of Dublin after 1922 *(National Library of Ireland).*

THE MOUNTJOY HEROES
*A Souvenir of the Great Hunger Strike. April 1920*

Top Row— J. O'Rourke. P. Lavery. A. Holt. J. O'Hagan. J. O'Neill. P. Shields. S. O'Carrol. D. Fitzpatrick. P. Molloy.
2nd — M. Molloy. P. Clynch. F. Loughran. M. Cooke. T. Tate. J. Larkin. P. O'Rourke. J. Burns. Phil. Shanahan. M.P.
3rd — M. Lynch. C. Andrews. P. Daly. P. Byrne. M. Crowe. (Leader) Councillor Carolan. M. Breen. M. Spillane. J. O'Neill. M. Lynam
P. Kean. M. Gleeson. O. Redmond. M. M°Coy. M. Gray. T. Smith

J. J. MOONEY  Photographer          7 Longwood Ave. DUBLIN.

■ Republican prisoners who took part in a hunger strike at Dublin Mountjoy Prison in April 1920, when large numbers of prisoners embarked on a rolling hunger strike in the prison (in which prisoners participated on a rotating basis). Hunger strikes were a common and potent weapon used by republican prisoners in the their struggle to be accorded what was essentially political status *(Military Archives)*.

Maurice Crowe of Tipperary and Michael Carolan of Belfast in hospital after the end of the Mountjoy hunger strike in April 1920 *(Military Archives).*

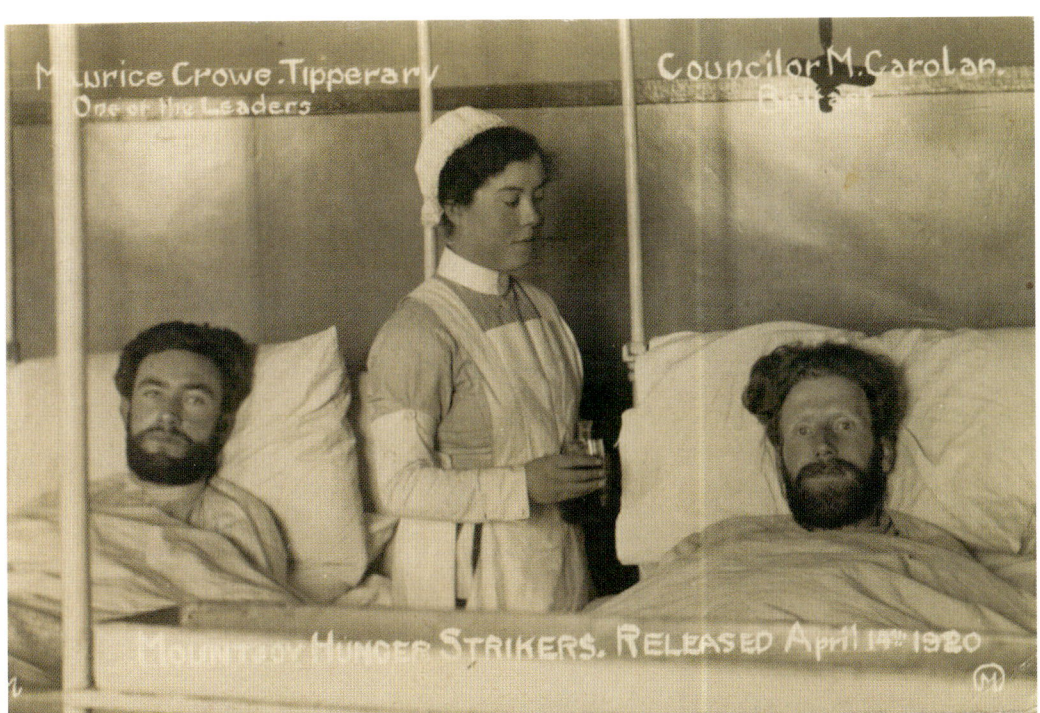

Protestors being held back by troops outside Mountjoy Prison, possibly during the April 1920 hunger strike *(Mercier Archives)*.

Three images of a raid by British forces on the Sinn Féin finance offices at 76 Harcourt Street, apparently in early 1920. This was a separate premises from the party headquarters, and had been purchased outright by Sinn Féin on the instructions of Michael Collins; the Dáil loan scheme was administered from here. The three men standing in the back of the truck are (l–r) Daniel J. O'Donovan, Sean O'Mahony and Dick McKee. The building is now occupied by the Irish Department of Foreign Affairs and Trade *(Military Archives)*.

■ British troops stop and search a car at the junction of Fleet Street and D'Olier Street. Such scenes became increasingly common as the conflict intensified, with curfews being imposed in Dublin from February 1920 onwards *(National Library of Ireland)*.

Prisoners being detained after a raid on an arms factory in Aungier Street, 22 February 1920. The IRA manufactured weapons, generally explosives, at a range of locations in Dublin *(National Library of Ireland)*.

■ 'TNT Mick': weapons being manufactured for the IRA at an unknown location. The identity of 'Mick' remains unclear, but the picture was taken by Joseph Cripps, a chemist and member of the Dublin Brigade of the IRA who was himself involved in manufacturing bombs *(Kilmainham Gaol Museum)*.

British troops and armoured cars during a raid in Dublin, seemingly on Aungier Street *(Military Archives)*.

■ Members of the Trinity College Dublin Officer Training Corps (OTC) take up positions as guards in Dublin Castle for the first time, on 17 March 1920. OTCs were first founded in British universities in 1907 to offer a fast track for students to become officers by allowing training whilst still a student. Trinity College set up its OTC in 1910 and it helped to 'defend' the campus during the Easter Rising. It was disbanded after the creation of the Irish Free State in 1922 *(National Library of Ireland)*.

British troops in the Royal Barracks (now Collins Barracks), *c.* 1920–21. Originally built in the first decade of the eighteenth century, it was the largest of the numerous military installations in Dublin used by the British armed forces. By June 1921 there were 11,412 troops in the Dublin District, though this extended across counties Cavan, Meath and Louth as well as Dublin, and not all of them would have been available for active service *(National Library of Ireland).*

■ The funeral of RIC District Inspector James Brady en route to Glasnevin Cemetery, October. Originally from Dublin and a veteran of the First World War, in which he had served in the Irish Guards and been a 'king's messenger' (i.e. a senior courier responsible for transporting messages from the king himself), he was killed in an IRA ambush in Sligo in September 1920. His coffin is draped in a union flag. Despite the prominence of the republican plot, Glasnevin Cemetery holds the graves of combatants from all sides of the Irish revolution, not to mention civilians *(National Library of Ireland)*.

An election poster for Walter Carpenter. Carpenter, from Dublin, had been a member of the Irish Citizen Army from its foundation and fought in the Easter Rising; here he is standing as a Labour candidate in the 1920 local elections. He was also a founder member of the Communist Party of Ireland and later served as president of the Irish Trade Union Congress, which later merged into the Irish Congress of Trade Unions *(National Library of Ireland)*.

## DUBLIN MUNICIPAL ELECTIONS, 1920.

### *Fitzwilliam, South City, Mansion House, and Royal Exchange Wards.*

REASONS why you should <u>VOTE</u> for

 WALTER CARPENTER

BECAUSE being a Worker he understands the needs and aspirations of the Working Class.

BECAUSE the freedom of the Working Class must be the work of the Working Class.

BECAUSE he stands for an Ireland owned and controlled by the Workers of Ireland, industrially as well as politically.

BECAUSE the Corporation have powers which can, and *must*, be used for the benefit of the Workers, and

**Carpenter,** if elected, will insist on those powers being put into operation.

BECAUSE a VOTE FOR **Carpenter** is a Vote for a Cleaner, Brighter, and Happier City.

THE LABOUR CANDIDATE.

REMEMBER THAT CARPENTER was the man who exposed the Slum Landlords and brought to light the Rebate of Rates Scandal at the Housing Inquiry during the Great Strike of 1913.

THEREFORE VOTE FOR CARPENTER, and assist him in his fight for the Political and Economic Freedom of the Irish Workers.

## VOTE FOR  CARPENTER

General Secretary, International Tailors, Machinists, and Pressers' Trade Union (Affiliated to the Irish Labour Party and Trade Union Congress, and the James Connolly Labour College).

CENTRAL COMMITTEE ROOMS, 44 YORK STREET, DUBLIN.

Published by the Candidate, and Printed by West, T.U. Printer, Capel Street.

■ Cumann na mBan convention, October 1920. Originally a female adjunct to the pre-1916 Irish Volunteers (the forerunners of the IRA), Cumann na mBan evolved into a significant organisation in its own right, and was the principal vehicle for the involvement of women in the independence movement. This convention was held in rooms behind the Carmelite church on Whitefriar Street; those attending entered via the church itself under the guise of a sodality, to avoid suspicion *(National Library of Ireland)*.

A memorial card for the eighteen-year-old IRA volunteer Kevin Barry. ▶ Barry was a student in University College Dublin when, on 20 September 1920, he and a number of others ambushed a group of British soldiers, who were collecting bread at Patrick Monk's bakery on Church Street, in order to steal their weapons. One solder was killed and two were fatally wounded, while Barry was captured as he hid beneath a lorry. He was the first member of the IRA to be captured carrying out an attack since the Easter Rising; despite his youth, on 20 October 1920 he was hanged in Mountjoy Prison and became the first republican to be executed under new and draconion laws directed against the IRA. His death at such a young age, despite a campaign for clemency, made him one of the most famous republican martyrs of the war *(Kilmainham Gaol Museum)*.

KEVIN G. BARRY
DIED FOR IRELAND NOV 1ST 1920.

A *c.* 1920 street scene on Church Street, near where Kevin Barry was arrested. This area of Dublin was quite impoverished and was characterised by extensive slum tenements. The poverty of the district had been noted as early as the 1840s and in September 1913 two tenement houses collapsed on the street, resulting in the deaths of seven people. A subsequent inquiry had held out the prospect of official action to tackle slum conditions in the city, but the outbreak of the First World War ensured that little progress was made *(National Library of Ireland)*.

Crowds outside the Royal Exchange Hotel on Parliament Street, after the killing on 22 September of John A. Lynch, a Sinn Féin councillor in Limerick who was in Dublin to deliver monies collected under the auspices of the Dáil loan. His lodgings were raided by British forces and he was shot dead. He may have been mistaken for the Cork IRA leader Liam Lynch. The official story was that he was killed while resisting arrest, but this claim was commonly made after extrajudicial killings by the British *(National Library of Ireland)*.

■ The body of the Tipperary IRA fighter Sean Treacy on Talbot Street, after his death in an exchange of gunfire with British forces. Treacy, with Dan Breen, had been involved in the Soloheadbeg ambush of 21 January 1919, at the beginning of the War of Independence. Both he and Breen were increasingly active in Dublin, and on 14 October 1920 Treacy was shot dead after he was spotted during a raid on the Republican Outfitters on Talbot Street. The shop was owned by Peadar Clancy of the Dublin Brigade of the IRA, who was a draper by trade; it was (perhaps inevitably, given its name) a well-known haunt of republicans *(Mercier Archives)*.

A ticket for the match played between Dublin and Tipperary on 21 November 1920: 'Bloody Sunday'. On the morning of Sunday 21 November the Dublin IRA, whose numbers had been augmented by other IRA members from outside the city, shot dead fourteen suspected and actual British military intelligence officers in the their lodgings around the city, and wounded a number of others, mainly in the south inner city. British forces later targeted the crowds attending a challenge football match being played by Dublin and Tipperary at Croke Park as part of the citywide crackdown that followed. Spectators were fired on from the Canal End of the ground and a number of people were shot dead. In the ensuing stampede, some were crushed and trampled to death; another was fatally impaled as he tried to clamber over a railing to escape. Nine were killed on the day, and five more died of wounds later; three of the dead were aged under fourteen *(GAA Museum)*.

Cumann na 5cleas lúiṫ nġaeḋealaċ
(GAELIC ATHLETIC ASSOCIATION)

# GREAT CHALLENGE MATCH
## (FOOTBALL)

# Tipperary v. Dublin

AT CROKE PARK
On SUNDAY, NOVEMBER 21, 1920
MATCH AT 2.45 P.M.

ADMISSION                    ∴ ∴ ∴ ∴ 1/-

44127

◄ Michael Hogan, the Tipperary captain and full back who was shot dead on the pitch. Ironically, he was a member of the IRA in Tipperary, though his death was due to the indiscriminate shooting. The Hogan Stand in Croke Park is named after him *(GAA Museum)*.

■ Croke Park, photographed the day after Bloody Sunday. Very few games were played in the ground between Bloody Sunday and the truce of July 1921; the GAA was spared bankruptcy by a loan from the Dáil *(National Library of Ireland)*.

Dick McKee. Born in Dublin and a printer by trade, McKee fought in the Easter Rising and eventually became Officer Commanding the Dublin Brigade of the IRA. He was responsible for many of their operations, including the attack on Lord French. He was captured, along with his fellow IRA member Peadar Clancy and a civilian, Conor Clune, in a British raid the night before Bloody Sunday; all three were killed whilst in captivity that night, presumably as a reprisal. The official version of events claimed they were shot while trying to escape; the bodies, however, apparently showed signs of torture *(Military Archives)*.

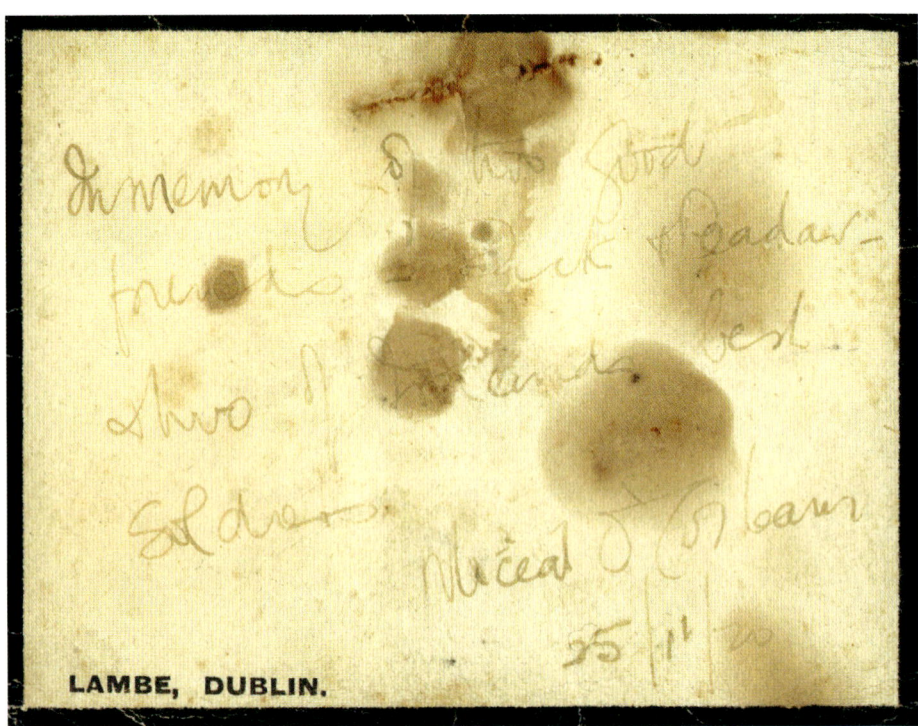

■ The back of the memorial card for Dick McKee, signed by Michael Collins. It reads: In memory of two good friends – Dick & Peadar – and two of Ireland's best soldiers. Míceál Ó Coileann, 25/11/20. Collins insisted on attending the funeral of both men. Members of the IRA subsequently raided the offices of the *Evening Herald* newspaper after it published a picture of Collins in the cortège as it made its way to Glasnevin, and they confiscated as many copies of the edition in question as possible across the city, lest the image be used by the British to identify Collins *(Kilmainham Gaol Museum)*.

Troops and family members in the grounds of Jervis Street hospital for one of the two military inquiries into the Bloody Sunday killings, 24 November 1920 (the other inquiry was held in the Mater Hospital). The overall conclusion of both was that the British forces had returned fire after being fired upon, which inevitably challenged the idea that it had been a reprisal. The reports did, however, conclude that members of the RIC had fired indiscriminately, which conveniently exonerated both the regular British army and paramilitary Auxiliary Cadets, who had also been involved in the raid on the ground. The findings were not made public at the time, but these dubious official conclusions were contradicted by copious eyewitness testimonies from civilians who were present *(National Library of Ireland)*.

British troops take over Dublin City Hall in December 1920. Originally opened as the Royal Exchange in 1779, it had served as the City Hall since 1852 and was requisitioned for use after British patience had worn thin with the nationalist sympathies of Dublin Corporation; indeed, a number of suspects had been captured in a British raid on City Hall a few weeks previously *(Dublin City Library and Archives, Birth of the Republic Collection).*

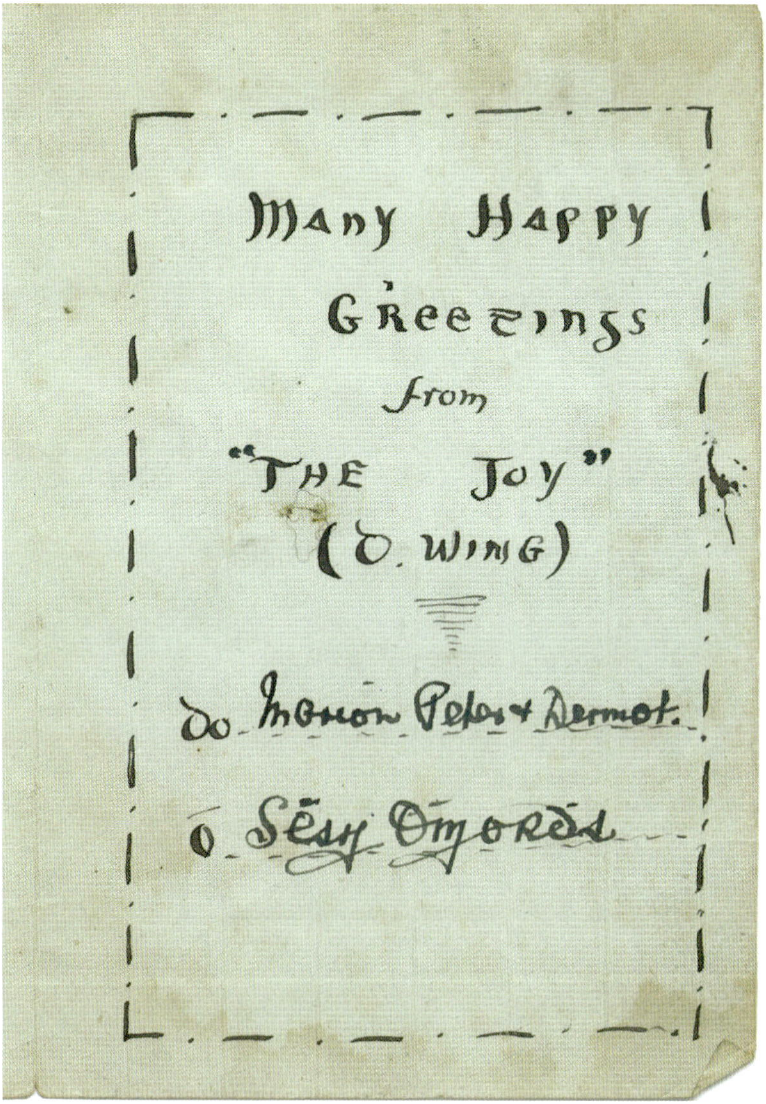

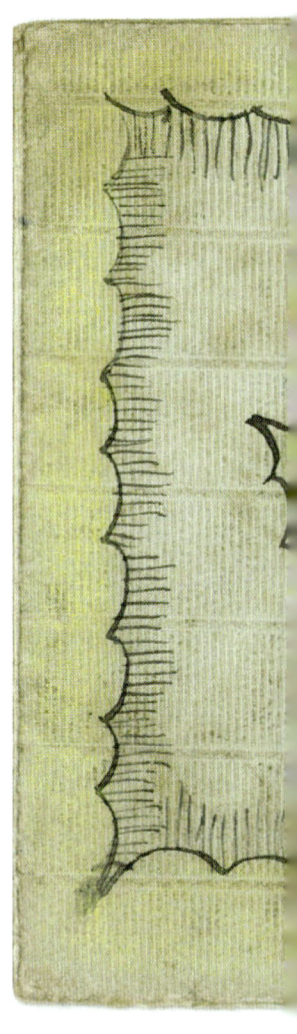

Many Happy
Greetings
from
"The Joy"
(D. Wing)

do Mánion Peter & Dermot.

ó Séan Ómórás

■ A hand-made Christmas card from Séan Ó Mordha, who was imprisoned on 'D' Wing in Mountjoy Prison *(Kilmainham Gaol Museum)*.

Every Good Wish for Christmastide

and the Coming New Year.

From

*Charles*

5th Armoured Car Coy.,
Marlborough Barracks,
Dublin.

Another Christmas card, this time from the British Army. Marlborough Barracks is now McKee Barracks *(Conor Dodd)*.

Damage to the interior of 21 Dawson Street after a British raid on 31 December. This flat was the home of Eileen McGrane of Cumann na mBan. The apartment also contained an office that was used by Michael Collins and others. Weapons and documents were seized in the raid, and McGrane herself was imprisoned, though she was still living at 21 Dawson Street when the Civil War broke out in June 1922 *(Military Archives).*

A driving permit issued by the British authorities under the 1920 Restoration of Order in Ireland Act. *(Dublin City Library and Archive, Birth of the Republic Collection).*

Passengers disembarking from a train at Westland Row (now Pearse) station, with Auxiliaries visible on the platform to the right. The Auxiliaries and the separate special constabulary (nicknamed Black and Tans) were paramilitary police recruited from the summer of 1920 onwards from ex-servicemen to bolster the ranks of the Dublin Metropolitan Police and Royal Irish Constabulary, and who acquired an enduring reputation for indiscipline and brutality *(Mercier Archives)*.

■ A crowd scatters as detachments of troops and Auxiliaries suddenly arrive at the junction of Middle Abbey Street and O'Connell Street (which was still officially called Sackville Street at this time), *c.* 1921 *(Getty Images)*.

■ Soldiers questioning a civilian in
a Dublin park, c. 1921 (Mercier
Archives).

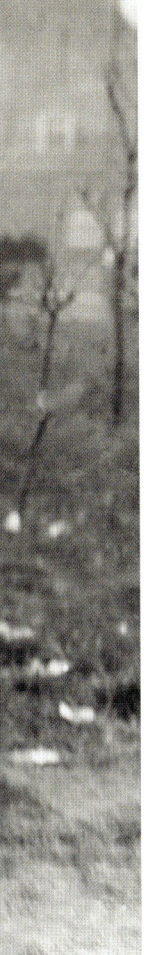

IRA prisoners in Kilmainham
Gaol pose for a photo, *c.* 1921
*(Kilmainham Gaol Museum).*

Two men in court dress in Dublin Castle, which since the Middle Ages had served as the headquarters of the British administrations that ruled Ireland. Such outfits were obligatory for civil servants attending state functions in the castle *(National Library of Ireland)*.

Sir John French inspecting troops in the upper yard of Dublin Castle, 1921 *(National Library of Ireland)*.

■ Thomas Whelan and Patrick Moran in Mountjoy Prison, seemingly enjoying cordial relations with an Auxiliary prior to being hanged on 14 March 1921 for their alleged involvement in the Bloody Sunday killings. The images were apparently smuggled out of the prison by Arthur Griffith, the journalist and founder of Sinn Féin, who was also imprisoned in Mountjoy at the time. Both men were buried in Mountjoy; they (and other executed prisoners such as Kevin Barry) were reinterred in Glasnevin Cemetery in 2001 *(Kilmainham Gaol Museum)*.

PATRICK MORAN

DIED FOR IRELAND MAR, 14TH 1921

■ A memorial card for Patrick Moran
*(Kilmainham Gaol Museum)*.

LEO   FITZGERALD,   I. R. A.

B. Coy. III Battalion Dublin Brigade.

Killed in Action in Great Brunswick Street
14th March, 1921.

ar veis vé go raib a anam.

A memorial card for Leo Fitzgerald, who was killed in a lengthy gun battle with British forces on Great Brunswick Street (now Pearse Street) on the night of the executions of Whelan and Moran. The fighting broke out in the vicinity of the current Dublin City Library and Archive, as Auxiliaries were rushing to the scene of an IRA bomb attack on the Dublin Metropolitan Police (DMP) station near Trinity College *(Kilmainham Gaol Museum).*

A battering ram attached to a tank is used to break down the door of the Johnston, Mooney and O'Brien bakery during a raid on Capel Street, *c.* 1921 *(Getty Images).*

The aftermath of an IRA attack on the London North Western Hotel on North Wall, 11 April 1921. This was the HQ of Q Company of the Auxiliary Division, who were tasked with patrolling the docks and rail lines. Grenades and paraffin were thrown into the building, though many of the grenades did not explode; the broken windows are clearly visible in the image above, while in the facing image a British officer and two Auxiliaries display some of the unexploded grenades that were used. One IRA member was killed in the exchange of gunfire that followed *(National Library of Ireland)*.

■ Some of the same cadets confiscate a motorcycle
on O'Connell Street *(National Library of Ireland).*

The burning of the Custom House, 25 May 1921. Designed by James Gandon and opened in 1785, this was one of the finest Georgian buildings in Dublin. It was targeted by the Dublin Brigade of the IRA primarily as a propaganda exercise; the fact that it housed the Local Government Board for Ireland was an added bonus. The IRA used paraffin and scrap fabric to start the blaze; the operation resulted in the deaths of five IRA members, as well as the capture of more than 80 *(Mercier Archives).*

The Custom House fire seen from the south side
of the Liffey. Note the porter barrels on the quays
*(National Library of Ireland).*

A horse-drawn fire tender belonging to Dublin Fire Brigade approaches the Custom House. The effectiveness of the fire brigade was diminished by the fact that many of the firemen were themselves members of the IRA and were not inclined to tackle a blaze started by their colleagues; some went so far as to smuggle weapons and other IRA members out of the burning building *(Michael Ward)*.

■ A member of the Royal Army Medical Corps stands over the body of an IRA member on Beresford Place, outside the Custom House *(Mercier Archives)*.

British regular troops and Auxiliaries examining captured weapons on Beresford Place. Note the prisoners in the background *(Mercier Archives).*

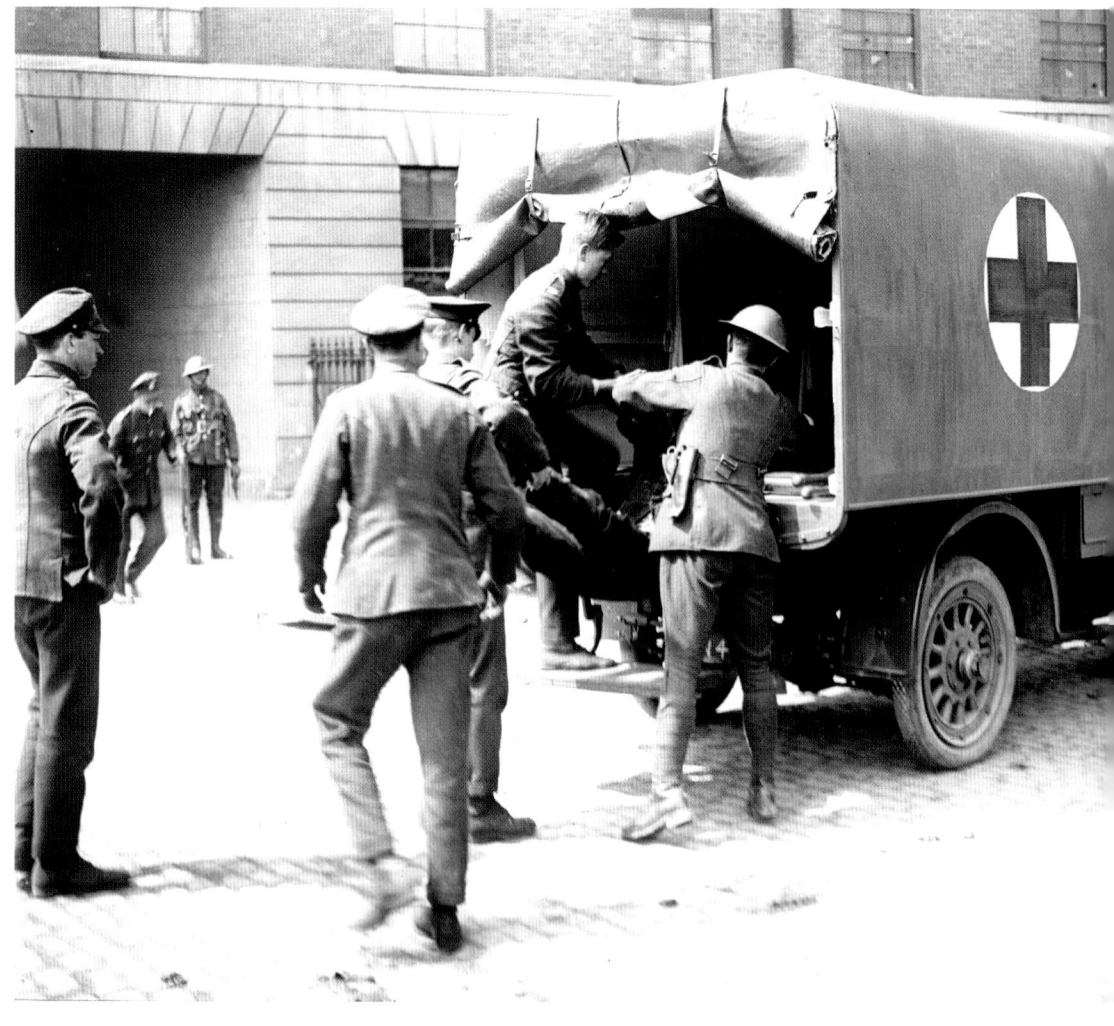

■ Soldiers load the body of one of those killed into
a military ambulance *(Mercier Archives)*.

IRA prisoners surrender after the attack on the Custom House *(Kilmainham Gaol Museum).*

■ Civilians under guard in the aftermath of the attack on the Custom House *(National Library of Ireland)*.

The ruined dome of the Custom House after the fire. It was rebuilt in the 1920s, though not with the original Portland stone, which came from Dorset, and the use of 'English' stone was seen as incongruous in the independent Ireland of the 1920s. Limestone from Kildare was used instead, which ensures that the rebuilt sections of the building are visibly darker than the original structure *(National Library of Ireland)*.

IRISH PEACE CONFERENCE, JULY, 1921.    Gathering at the Mansion House.

E. & S. Ltd., Dublin]                                                    Photo, Hogan, Dublin.

IRISH PEACE CONFERENCE, JULY, 1921.    Reciting the Rosary outside Mansion House.

E. & S. Ltd., Dublin]                                                    [Photo, Hogan, Dublin

■ Four postcards of the scenes outside the Mansion House on 8 July 1921 for the second meeting of a peace conference called by the Lord Mayor, Laurence O'Neill, which was attended by Sinn Féin and southern unionists, amongst others. A key item on its agenda was the negotiation of a truce between the British and the IRA and, to that end, the British General Officer Commanding in Ireland, General Neville Macready, attended in person; he did so, armed with a pistol *(Military Archives)*.

IRISH PEACE CONFERENCE, JULY, 1921. Gathering at the Mansion House.
E. & S. Ltd., Dublin]                                    [Photo, Hogan, Dublin

IRISH PEACE CONFERENCE, JULY, 1921. General Macready entering Mansion House with Lord Mayor.
E. & S. Ltd., Dublin]                                    [Photo, Hogan, Dublin

IRISH PEACE CONFERENCE, JULY, 1921.
Truce Day, July 11th, 1921.

E. & S. Ltd., Dublin]                                    [Photo, Hogan, Dublin

■ A toddler with a flag (presumably a tricolour) in an unidentified
location on 11 July 1921, the day that the truce came into effect
*(Military Archives).*

Children waving tricolours to mark the truce of 11 July 1921 at an unidentified location in the city; note the lack of footwear *(Kilmainham Gaol Museum)*.

The POLICE have ORDERS
to prevent all Carts, Spring Vans
& Vehicles of every kind
Excepting
Gentlemens Carriages & occupied
Hack Cars & Cabs from passing
through the Lower Castle Yard

Civilians, Auxiliaries, soldiers and a dog can be seen outside the gate to Dublin Castle's lower yard on the day of the truce in expectation of an announcement. The Olympia Theatre is visible in the background (top, facing page), and some of the interactions seem surprisingly cordial *(Mercier Archives)*.

IRISH PEACE CONFERENCE, JULY, 1921.    Delegates leaving Dun Laoghaire.

E. & S. Ltd., Dublin]      [Photo, Hogan, Dublin.

▪ Delegates about to depart from Dún Laoghaire for preliminary negotiations with the British government in London, July 1921. (L–r): Arthur Griffith, Erskine Childers, Éamon de Valera, Count George Plunkett, Eamonn Duggan *(Military Archives)*.

A public session of the second Dáil Eireann in the Mansion House in the changed climate of August 1921. A key item on its agenda was the prospect of negotiations with the British on a political settlement of some kind *(National Library of Ireland)*.

■ A remarkable bird's-eye shot from the top of the Nelson Pillar on O'Connell Street, *c.* 1921, presumably after a rally or public meeting. Note the car to the right; the figure in the back seat may be Éamon de Valera *(National Library of Ireland)*.

Members of Dáil Éireann – TDs – leaving the Mansion House on the second day of the Dáil session, 17 August. (L–r): Margaret Pearse, Frank Lawless and Margaret Mary Pearse; the two Pearses were, respectively, the sister and mother of the executed 1916 leaders Patrick and Willie Pearse *(National Library of Ireland)*.

■ Sean MacEoin, in uniform on the right, a prominent and successful IRA leader (and TD) in his native Longford, walks across the pitch of Croke Park during a match being held during the truce *(Military Archives)*.

Michael Collins greets the Kilkenny and Dublin hurlers in Croke Park, prior to the Leinster Hurling final of 11 September 1921, which had been delayed due to the ongoing conflict *(National Library of Ireland)*.

■ Collins shakes the hand of Alderman James Nowlan of Kilkenny (after whom Kilkenny's Nowlan Park is named) on the day of the Leinster Hurling Final, 11 September 1921. Harry Boland – a former Dublin hurler himself – is visible on the left *(National Library of Ireland)*.

Our Lady of Perpetual Succour ('Patroness to the IRA'), made by IRA prisoners in Kilmainham in August 1921; many prisoners remained in custody for a period after the truce *(Kilmainham Gaol Museum).*

# Dante Sexcentenary Celebration

Promoted by

## The Ministry of Fine Arts, Dail Eireann

— WILL BE HELD IN THE —

## Mansion House, Dublin, on Tuesday, 6th December, 1921, at 7.30 p.m.

ADMIT BEARER

■ A ticket to an exhibition on the medieval Italian poet Dante Alighieri, author of the legendary epic *Commedia* (usually known as *The Divine Comedy*), organised by Dáil Éireann, a small indication that the Dáil attempted to carry out a wide range of functions befitting a formal government. It is dated 6 December 1921, the same day on which the Anglo-Irish Treaty was signed in London *(National Library of Ireland)*.

A crowd outside the university buildings on Earlsfort Terrace during the Dáil
debate on the Anglo-Irish Treaty between December 1921 and January 1922. The
terms of the Treaty, which held out the prospect of Ireland becoming a 26-county
dominion within the British Empire, rather than an independent republic, proved
deeply repugnant to many in the independence movement. The Dáil sessions
that met to debate on whether or not to accept it proved acrimonious *(National
Library of Ireland)*.

The council chamber in Earlsfort Terrace in which the Treaty debates took place *(National Library of Ireland)*.

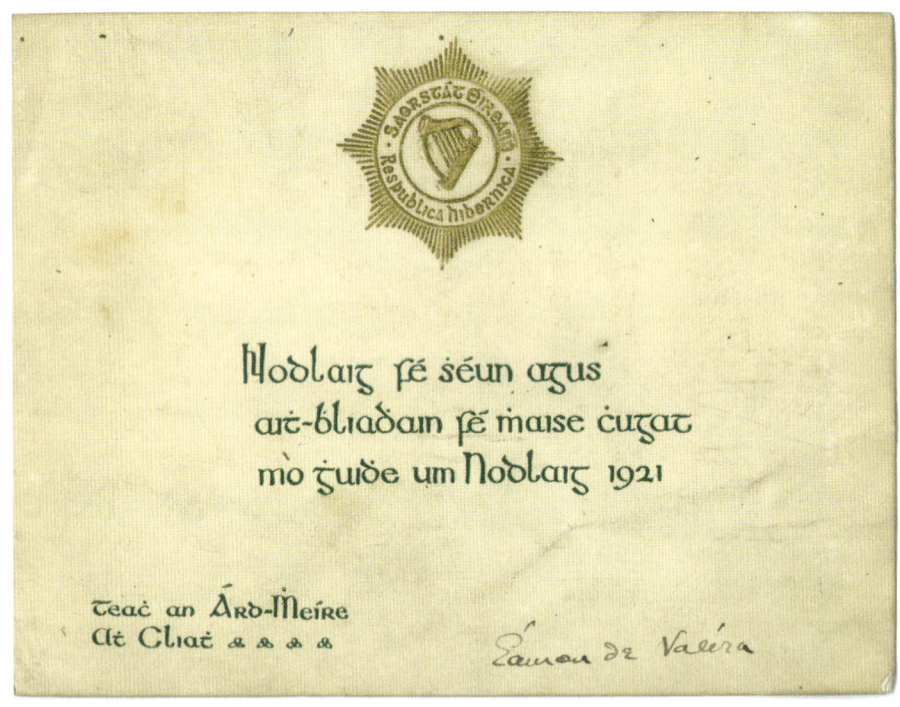

'Any day in Dublin', a cartoon by 'Shemus', aka Ernest Forbes, published
in *The Freeman's Journal* of 30 December 1921. Given the ongoing
uncertainty over Ireland's political future, the Dublin of the truce
remained a surprisingly lawless place, a reality that is perhaps reflected
in the cartoon *(National Library of Ireland)*.

# 1922

A car carrying Michael Collins, head of the new Provisional Government established under the Treaty, arrives at Dublin Castle for the handover of power by the outgoing British administration, 16 January 1922. The Dáil ratified the Treaty amidst great acrimony on 7 January, and Collins became head of the Provisional Government that oversaw the transition to independence and the creation of the Irish Free State. Both Sinn Féin and the IRA split over the terms of the Treaty, with Collins emerging as the figurehead of the pro-Treaty faction *(Mercier Archives).*

Goodbye Dublin: British troops mark their departure from
Dublin, though the soldier actually writing the slogan was
apparently from Belfast. British forces began to withdraw
rapidly from southern Ireland in early 1922, with many
earmarked for duties across the post-war British Empire
(National Library of Ireland).

■ British soldiers buy fruit from street vendors prior to their
departure from Dublin. The Tommy on the far left seems to
be hoping his charm might work on one of them. *(National
Library of Ireland).*

Troops from a Scottish regiment transporting material for departure on the Dublin quays, January 1922 *(Mercier Archives).*

■ The ratification of the Treaty saw the Provisional Government establish a formal military force, based around those members of the IRA who supported the Treaty. Here, members of the new 'National Army' march to take over Beggars Bush Barracks from the outgoing British garrison, 2 February 1922. The new army were provided with weapons and material by the British government of David Lloyd George *(National Library of Ireland)*.

Richard Mulcahy, former Chief of Staff of the IRA and now Minister for Defence in the new Provisional Government, inspects troops of the National Army in Beggars Bush Barracks, January 1922. This was one of the first barracks handed over by the British Army as it withdrew. It was later the venue for a number of executions of republicans by the National Army (including that of Erskine Childers) in the eventual Civil War *(Mercier Archives)*.

■ The committee responsible for drafting the new Free State constitution in Dublin's Shelbourne Hotel. Third from right is Hugh Kennedy, legal officer to the Provisional Government and future Chief Justice of the Free State *(National Library of Ireland)*.

Count George Plunkett (the father of the executed 1916 leader Joseph Mary Plunkett and formerly the Dáil's Minister for Foreign Affairs) addresses an anti-Treaty rally in O'Connell Street, February 1922 *(Mercier Archives)*.

Michael Collins addresses a pro-Treaty rally on Westmoreland Street, outside the Bank of Ireland, March 1922 *(Mercier Archives)*.

The National Army take over guard duties at the Bank of Ireland's headquarters on College Green, March 1922. The Bank of Ireland, founded in 1783, had been the official bank of the British administration in Ireland (hence the presence of a guard at its headquarters). While its management were politically unionist, Michael Collins had invited it to serve in a similar role for the new Free State; this was accepted and the National Army took over the guard duties. The building had opened in 1731 to house the Irish parliament that was later abolished by the 1801 Act of Union, but despite its symbolism, the Free State was in no position to purchase it as the venue for the Dáil *(Mercier Archives)*.

The National Army parade outside the Bank of Ireland,
March 1922 *(Military Archives)*.

An Easter Rising commemoration, possibly on Sackville Street, April 1922. The banner indicates that these were members of 'E' Company of the Fourth Battalion of the Irish Volunteers (the forerunner to the IRA); this was one of the units under the command of Éamonn Ceannt that was active in the south-west inner city, and which seized the South Dublin Union and other buildings in that area. While veterans of the Rising formed the core of the independence movement, many remained neutral during the eventual civil war that broke out in June 1922. *(Mercier Archives).*

A poster for voter registration organised by the Dublin Workers' Council. In February 1918 the Representation of the People Act and Redistribution of Seats Act had passed the UK parliament and extended the electoral franchise to all men over 21 and most women over 30; the Free State then extended voting rights to all women over the age of 21 *(National Library of Ireland)*.

# Cnám

## cumann na mban

THE OFFICIAL PAPER OF THE ORGANISATION.

Vol. 1 No. 2     Aibreán, 1922.     PRICE TWOPENCE.

## STÁIR NA h-ÉIREANN.

"Leanfaimíd ne an lochrann
  Do las ár sinnsir romhainn,
Is ní heagal linn go bhfeódhfaidh
  a geró 'nár ndéidh."
            (Amhrán Dóchais).

Sin é díreach an obair atá la deanamh againn i gCumann na mBan Cumainn iols ar ndícheall do dheanamh chumh saoirse iomlán do bhaint amach d' ár dtír féin. Caithimid sprid na saoirse do choimeád ar lasadh n' ár gcróidhe féin ma's mian linn aon obair fóghanta a dheánamh. Dá bhrí son ba mhaith an rud é, go mór mór i lathair na h-uaire feáchaint siar beagaínín ar stáir na tíre seo. Is munic adeirtear go bhfhuil sé ana-dheacair cursaí politióchta an lae indhui do thuisgint ach, dar ndó, sé ár dtuairim láidir da mbeadh eolus cruinn againn ar thréithibh na nGall i gcursai cogaidh, agus i gcursaí politióchta ó thanadar go dtí an tir seo, ní fada a leanfhad na mearbhall san ar ár n. aigne. Ní h. í seo an ceúd uair ag Sasana ag tabhairt fé sinne do dhalladh le bladar nó le gheallúinti bhreaghtha, nuair atá teipithe uirthe glan sinne do chur fé smacht le neart airm.

Rud eile dhe, molaimídne do gach aon bhall de Cumann na mBán stuidéir a dheanamh ar stáir mar is mó agus is tabhachtach an tairbhe tisethaidh as dí fhéin. Níl aon slíghe cile athá níos fearr chumh misneach a thabhairt di. Cidhfheadh sí gurb iad na daoine is mo clú agus is mo teist i n-Eirinn indiù, ná, na daoine nár gheill riamh do Shasana, na daoine a thuig na beádh sos ná suaimneas go deo againn go dtí go mbeidh an dha naisúin deighilte amach ó n-a cheile ar fad Sid iad Art Mór Mac Murchadha,

Tone, Emmet agus na céadta eile. Nior staonadar siúd, ní staonfaimid ne ach oiread, má dhéinimid aithris ortha siúd.

"Neart is brí na h-óige
  D'ar dtarrach tríd a gcomhlann
Is bainfimíd ne an céo so
  Do phór na dtréan."
                 CONÁIN
                 Phís Herbert, ş.

\*\*\*

## BELFAST AND ITS SIGNIFICANCE

All our minds and hearts have been fixed on Belfast and the terrible happenings there, and now we are told "Peace has been declared," and the various articles of that "Peace" are laid before us. The daily Press are loud in their praise for that "Peace." Various persons, important and unimportant, are uttering encomiums thereon, and we of Cumann na mBan may usefully examine the situation and look the truth in the face.

The North-Eastern Counties of Ireland have been a source of trouble for a very long time. In every other part of Ireland the settlers who came over from England or Scotland were absorbed in the native population and became "more Irish than the Irish themselves"— "Hiberniores Hibernicis ipsis," as Spencer called them. And not even the stringent punishments of the Statute of Kilkenny were able to prevent this absorption.

In the North-East, however, the case was different. The native population was practically exterminated from a large part of Ulster, and by the process of planting whole families, and giving estates on condition that no Irish or

(Continued on page 3.)

An April 1922 edition of the official Cumann na mBan newspaper. The leadership of the organisation and many of the rank and file opposed the Treaty; the divisions over whether or not to accept permeated virtually all nationalist and republican groups (*Dublin City Library and Archive, Birth of the Republic Collection*).

■ A note informing the citizens of Dublin about unauthorised persons obtaining goods under the false pretence of supporting the Belfast boycott. The boycott had begun in September 1920 in response to sectarian attacks in Northern Ireland. It was largely ineffective, but was seized on with vigour as a public policy by the anti-Treaty IRA in the lead-up to the Civil War *(National Library of Ireland)*.

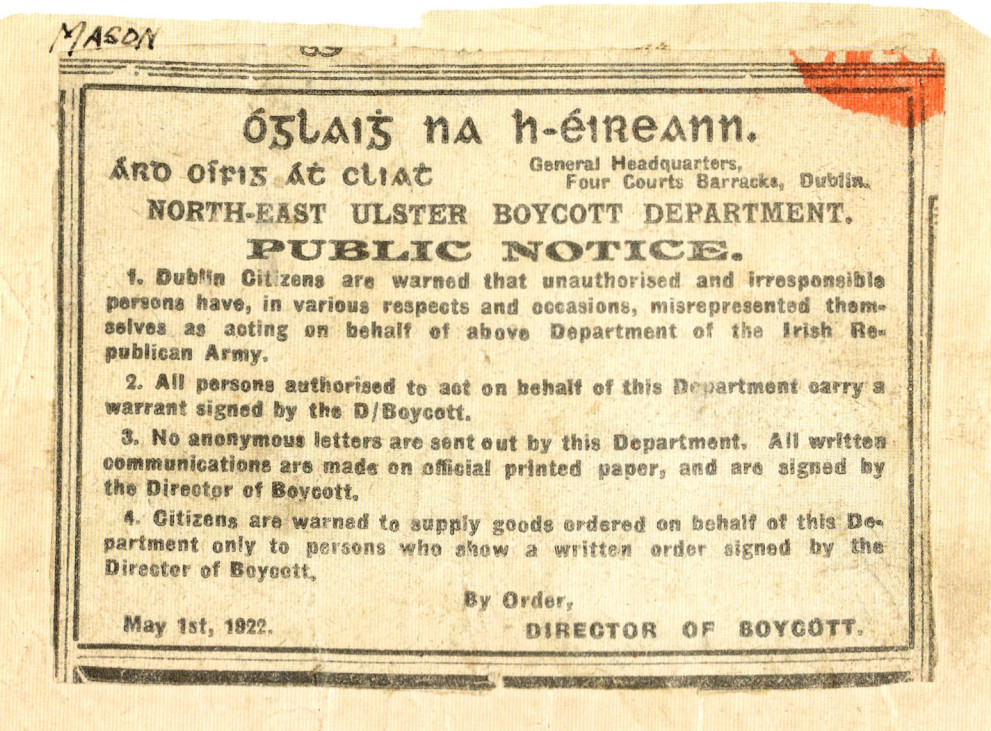

MASON

## Óglaiġ na h-Éireann.

ÁRO OIFIS ÁT CLIAT

General Headquarters,
Four Courts Barracks, Dublin.

### NORTH-EAST ULSTER BOYCOTT DEPARTMENT.

## PUBLIC NOTICE.

1. Dublin Citizens are warned that unauthorised and irresponsible persons have, in various respects and occasions, misrepresented themselves as acting on behalf of above Department of the Irish Republican Army.

2. All persons authorised to act on behalf of this Department carry a warrant signed by the D/Boycott.

3. No anonymous letters are sent out by this Department. All written communications are made on official printed paper, and are signed by the Director of Boycott.

4. Citizens are warned to supply goods ordered on behalf of this Department only to persons who show a written order signed by the Director of Boycott.

By Order,

May 1st, 1922.

DIRECTOR OF BOYCOTT.

A pro-Treaty pamphlet by Arthur Griffith. The founder in 1905 of Sinn Féin was best known as a prolific journalist and had headed the delegation that negotiated the Treaty in 1921 and replaced de Valera as president of the Dáil after the Treaty split. Along with Michael Collins, he was the most senior leader of the pro-Treaty side *(Dublin City Library and Archive, Birth of the Republic Collection)*. ▶

# ARGUMENTS FOR THE TREATY

## By ARTHUR GRIFFITH
President of Dail Eireann.

MARTIN LESTER, LIMITED
78 Harcourt Street    ::    Dublin

PRICE SIXPENCE.

■ The Dublin Faughs team became the All-Ireland hurling
champions 1920 when they beat a Cork team 4-9 to
4-3 in a final that had been delayed until 14 May 1922
due to the upheavals of the revolution *(GAA Museum).*

An anti-Treaty rally on O'Connell Street in early 1922; the speaker or speakers are unknown, though a tricolour is clearly visible *(Kilmainham Gaol Museum)*.

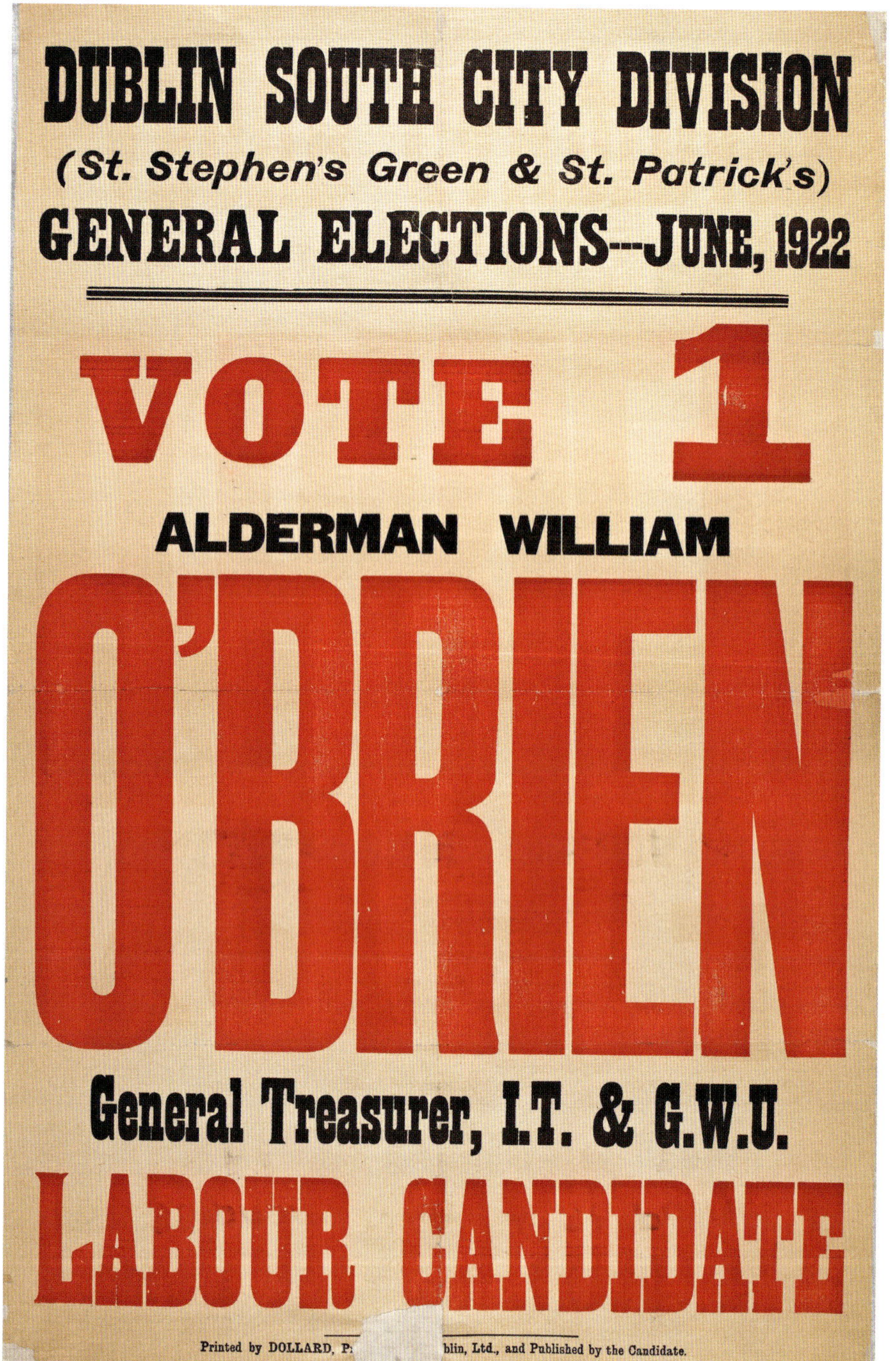

DUBLIN SOUTH CITY DIVISION
(St. Stephen's Green & St. Patrick's)
GENERAL ELECTIONS---JUNE, 1922

VOTE 1
ALDERMAN WILLIAM
O'BRIEN
General Treasurer, I.T. & G.W.U.
LABOUR CANDIDATE

Printed by DOLLARD, P: ... blin, Ltd., and Published by the Candidate.

◄ Election material for William O'Brien, future leader of the Irish Labour Party, at the June 1922 election. The socio-economic issues raised in the election extended far beyond just the constitutional status of the Free State, which was the key issue that led to Civil War between the pro- and anti-Treaty factions *(National Library of Ireland)*.

Joe McHenry of the IRA on the roof of the Four Courts. The ■ IRA had split over the terms of the Treaty, and the enormous Georgian Four Courts (the centrepiece of Ireland's legal system) was occupied by the faction most vociferously opposed to the Treaty in April 1922 *(Kilmainham Gaol Museum)*.

A famous propaganda image of the IRA patrolling Grafton Street very visibly in June 1922. By their nature, activities such as these were an implicit challenge to the authority of the Provisional Government. Note the youth of the IRA volunteers on the right of the picture; the organisation received many recruits during the truce who had played no role in the War of Independence and who were contemptuously dubbed 'Trucileers' by the Free State authorities *(Mercier Archives).*

The National Army attacks the Four Courts with artillery (borrowed from the
remaining British garrison) from the bottom of Winetavern Street, at the
outbreak of the Civil War between the anti-Treaty IRA and the Free State in June
1922. While the early months of 1922 had seen numerous attempts to broker
a compromise between the two sides, the British insisted on the Treaty being
fulfilled to the letter, and following the assassination by the IRA of Sir Henry
Wilson, the Irish-born former Chief of the Imperial General Staff, in London,
British patience snapped and Lloyd George's government insisted that it was
time for the Provisional Government under Collins to act. The Four Courts were
attacked by Free State forces on 28 June 1922 *(Mercier Archives)*.

■ Free State troops use artillery to fire on the Four Courts from the bottom of Bridgefoot Street *(National Library of Ireland).*

■ Crowds of civilians gather along the Liffey to watch the fighting at a safe distance. While the areas around the Four Courts and O'Connell Street saw action at the outset of the Civil War, and while fighting took place in other parts of Dublin, such as Aungier Street, large tracts of the city were left untouched. Just as had happened in the early phases of the Easter Rising of 1916, curious onlookers took to the streets of Dublin in droves during the fighting of June 1922 *(National Library of Ireland).*

The destruction of the Public Record Office in the Four Courts causes an enormous plume of smoke to rise into the sky. Vast quantities of irreplaceable official records that dated back to the medieval period were lost in the process. It had been used as an arms dump by the anti-Treaty garrison *(Military Archives)*.

THE MINE EXPLOSION IN THE FOUR COURTS, JUNE 30, 1922.

■ Smoke emerges from the dome of the Four Courts, presumably after the building was abandoned; note the figures standing in front of it *(Alamy)*.

The ruins of the Public Record Office, with the ■ wreck of a car visible amongst the rubble *(Irish Architectural Archive)*.

■ The ruins of the Four Courts, as seen from Arran Quay.
The fighting around the Four Courts and O'Connell
Street was the most destructive of the Civil War and, in
terms of the revolutionary period, was only rivalled by
the destruction caused by the Easter Rising of 1916 and
the burning of Cork in 1920. By the end of the Civil War
three of Dublin's most iconic Georgian public buildings –
the GPO, the Custom House and the Four Courts – lay in
ruins. All three were reconstructed after independence;
the Four Courts reopened in 1932 *(Military Archives)*.

A Free State armoured car (again supplied by the British) on Baggot Street, 29 June 1922, during a raid that resulted in the capture of IRA officer Leo Henderson (who had been in charge of the Belfast boycott). Note the insignia on the door of the vehicle *(National Library of Ireland)*.

# ADDRESS TO THE DUBLIN BRIGADE

BY THE OFFICER COMMANDING.

Officers and men of the Dublin Brigade of the Army of the Republic.

The General Command wishes me to express to you its appreciation of your bravery and your loyalty to the Republic.

Unnatural enemies, brother Irishmen, yielding to the threats of Britain and resolved to disestablish the Republic, made war upon you, the soldiers of the Republic, hoping by force to compel us all to share the disgrace of their cowardly surrender.

The position in which our comrades were attacked involved us in an action, unsuited to our organisation and our equipment but, by a series of magnificent rear-guard actions, made glorious by the stand and heroic death of Cathal Brugha, the Brigade has been able to disengage almost intact in personnel and material.

Those who would make us bend the knee to England's King have suffered severely and they will now know that they will not be permitted to destroy the Republic or surrender our national independence with impunity.

We can now at once revert to the tactics which made us invincible formerly and which can now equally ensure that the Republic of Tone and Emmet, of Pearse and Connolly, of McSwiney and Barry, of McKee and Clancy and of Cathal Brugha will not be supplanted by an alien monarchy.

Your comrades throughout the country are similarly in arms, inspired by the example you have set and which has been made memorable by the heroic death of Cathal Brugha. The young manhood and womanhood of Ireland are with us. Some have been misled, but their eyes are opening and they will soon recognise that it is not the will of the Irish people but the will of Britain that seeks the distruction of the Republic.

Sacrifices have yet to be made, tortures may have to be endured, but the glorious manner in which you have faced the onslaught of the past week raises a great hope that it is beyond the power of any man to sell this nation as a vassal state.

(Signed)          OSCAR TRAYNOR.
                  O/C Dublin Brigade.

An 'address to the Dublin Brigade' of the IRA, issued by Oscar Traynor, its commanding officer, on the outbreak of the Civil War; the name 'IRA' was retained by that segment of the organisation that opposed the Treaty *(Dublin City Library and Archive, Birth of the Republic Collection).*

Apart from the Four Courts, the other major theatre of conflict
in Dublin during the outbreak of the Civil War was in and around
O'Connell Street, the north-eastern part of which was occupied by
the anti-Treaty IRA. This terrace of buildings, which contained a
number of hotels, including the Gresham, was dubbed the 'Block'
by the republicans who occupied it. Here, Free State troops fire at
the buildings from the top of Henry Street, with the Nelson Pillar
in the background *(National Library of Ireland).*

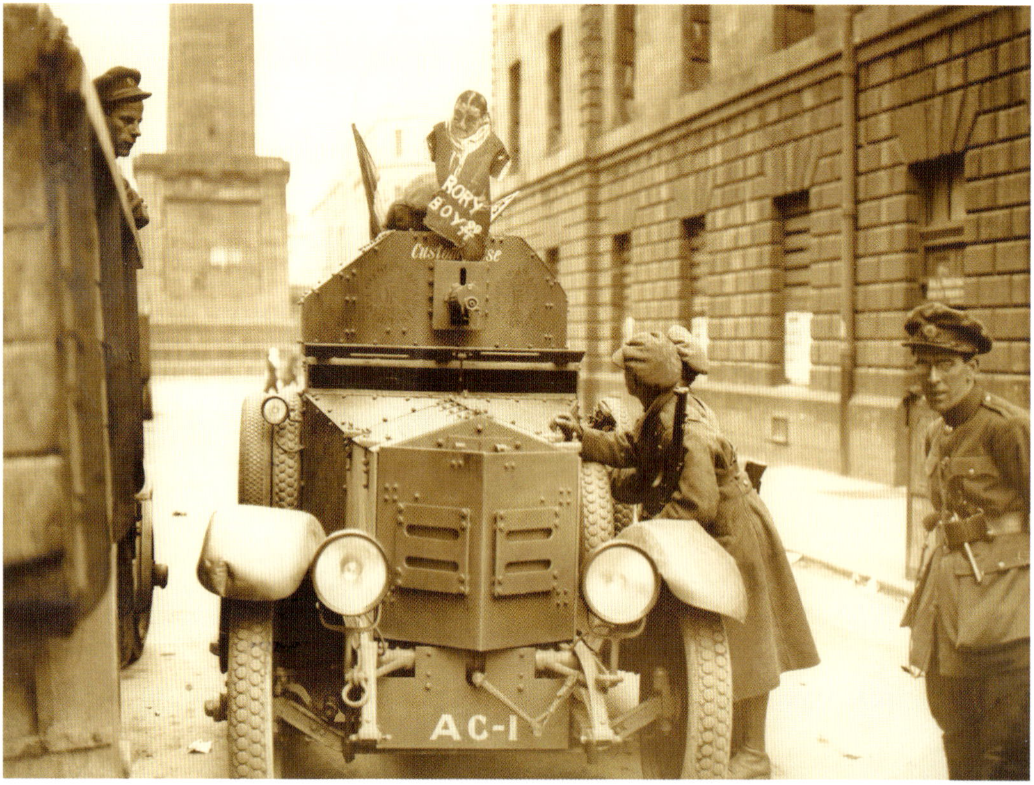
RORY
BOY
AC-1

HAMMOND No 4
LANE

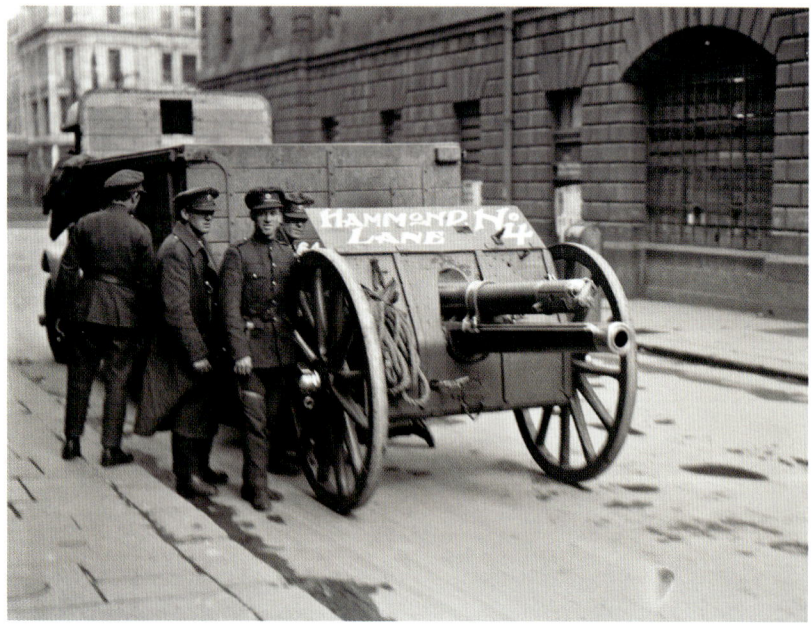

◄ A Free State armoured car at the top of Henry Street, adorned with what appears to be an effigy of the anti-Treaty IRA leader Rory O'Connor, who had commanded the garrison at the Four Courts *(National Library of Ireland)*.

Wounded members of the National Army during a lull in the fighting around O'Connell Street *(Mercier Archives)*. ▪

◄ Troops and an artillery piece outside the GPO, on Henry Street. Having been used against the Four Courts, artillery borrowed from the British was also used against the republican positions on O'Connell Street; it was manoeuvred into position at the top of Henry Street, using armoured cars for cover. The Gresham Hotel was particularly badly damaged by artillery *(National Library of Ireland)*.

National Army soldiers advance on the Gresham
Hotel, which had been seized by the IRA, during
the fighting *(Mercier Archives)*.

A Free State armoured car outside the 'Block' of
buildings on the north-east of O'Connell Street
*(Military Archives)*.

The burning shell of the 'Block' seized by the anti-Treaty forces, extending from North Earl Street to Findlater Place and including a number of hotels, with the extent of the damage clearly evident. By basing themselves here, the anti-Treaty IRA had ensured that the wide expanse of O'Connell Street effectively cut them off from their fellow anti-Treaty republicans in the Four Courts *(National Library of Ireland)*.

A contemporary postcard image of the same location, also taken by W.D. Hogan, a well-known commercial photographer based on Henry Street; note the difference in quality between this and the plate glass negative *(Kilmainham Gaol Museum)*.

E. & S., Ltd., D.]  Military Operations, Dublin, June-July, 1922.  [Photo, Hogan, D.
NATIONAL FORCES BOMBING HAMMAM HOTEL.

■ Pro-Treaty snipers at the top of Henry Street, in what is almost certainly a staged photo; the photographer would have been dangerously exposed to gunfire otherwise *(Mercier Archives)*.

Civilians leave the Edinburgh Hotel on O'Connell Street after the fighting had ended, having been confined there for a number of days *(National Library of Ireland)*.

E. & S., Ltd., D.]        Military Operations, Dublin, June–July, 1922.        [Photo. Hogan, Dublin.
**GENERAL VIEW UPPER O'CONNELL ST. AFTER SURRENDER.**

E. & S., Ltd., D.]

Contemporary postcard views of the ruins of O'Connell Street, complete with civilian onlookers *(Kilmainham Gaol Museum)*.

Military Operations, Dublin, June–July, 1922.　[Photo, Hogan, Dublin.

RUINS OF HAMMAM HOTEL, O'CONNELL ST.

■ Free State troops guarding a post office, presumably to prevent any looting amidst the disruption *(Mercier Archives)*.

Members of the Red Cross pose with a broken clock face at the top of Henry Street after the fighting had ended *(National Library of Ireland)*.

■ Fr Albert (Thomas Bibby) arrives on O'Connell Street to tend to the wounded. A member of the Capuchin congregation based on Church Street, near the Four Courts, Fr Albert and other friars had ministered to some of the leaders of the Easter Rising in captivity and retained close links to republicans. He had also ministered to anti-Treaty forces during the outbreak of the Civil War and had sought to act as an intermediary between them and the National Army, though such activities ensured he was subsequently the subject of an official complaint made to the Archbishop of Dublin *(National Library of Ireland)*.

An opening salvo in the propaganda war: a Free State poster condemning republicans for the destruction of the Four Courts. Note the use of the term 'irregular', chosen by the Free State to avoid giving any sense of legitimacy to their republican opponents *(Dublin City Library and Archive, Birth of the Republic collection).*

# DESTRUCTION OF FOUR COURTS

### WITH ALL ITS HISTORIC DOCUMENTS THROUGH FIRE CAUSED BY

## IRREGULARS' EXPLOSION OF MINE

The following was issued by G.H.Q., Irish Army, on the 4th July:—

### A CONNECTED MINE.

Those who were in the Hall of the Four Courts at the time of the Explosion are well aware that it was a Mine Exploded, *and that it was Connected.* Other Connected Mines have since been removed from the Four Courts. Our Men were in the Hall when the Explosion took place. At that time the Fire had not reached that part of the Building.

### NO SHELL.

No Shell came near that part of the Building while our Men were there.

### OTHER TRAPS TO KILL.

Other Traps were laid with the intention of Slaughtering our Troops *after their occupation of the Building,* but this was the only one that Succeeded. One of these Traps was a Mine concealed by a Typewriter Cover.

In a letter dated, June 29, addressed, "O.C. 5.," Mr. Oscar Traynor, a Leader of the Irregulars wrote : "Congratulations on your Mine. If you have no more of these let me know."

One of the Irregulars' Leaders, Mr. Ernest O'Malley assured Brigadier-Gen. O'Daly "That the Mine was Exploded by the Irregulars in the Four Courts". HE ALSO EX-PRESSED REGRET THAT THE CASUALTIES AMONG THE TROOPS WERE NOT GREATER.

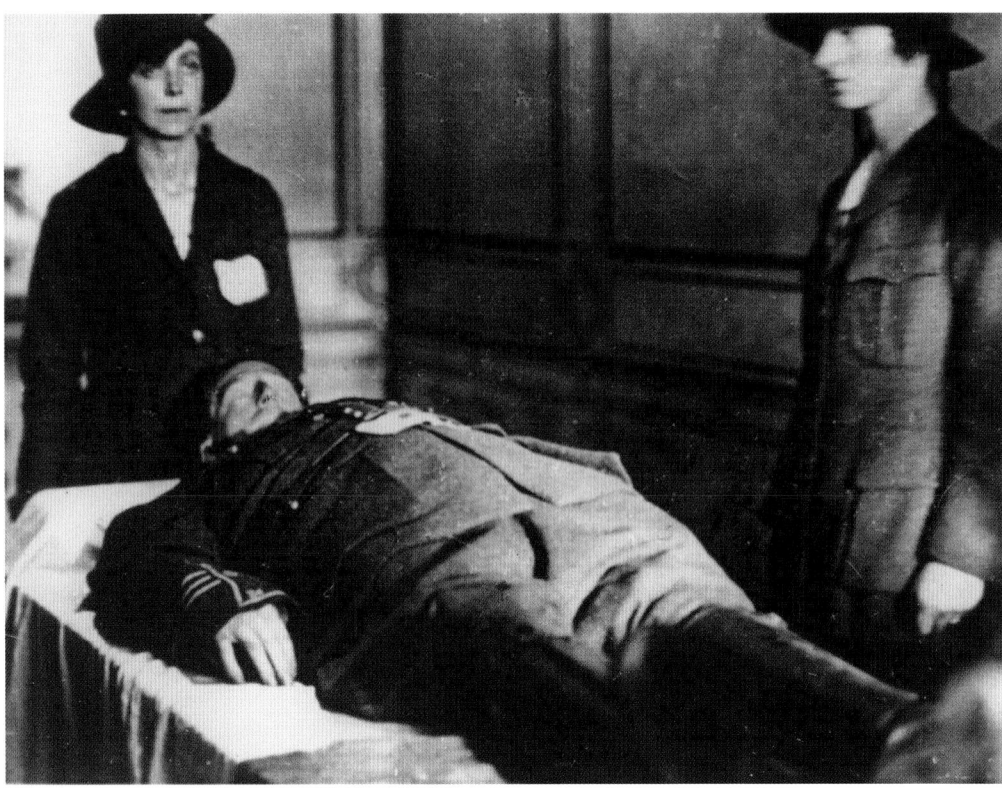

■ Cathal Brugha's body lying in hospital, flanked by members of Cumann na mBan. Brugha (born Charles Burgess) had fought in the South Dublin Union during the Easter Rising, displaying considerable courage and being severely wounded. Enormously respected for his bravery, he had served as Minister for Defence in the Dáil government though he disapproved of some of the methods advocated by Collins. Having taken the anti-Treaty side, he was fatally wounded by Free State forces as he ran out of the Granville Hotel firing his pistol *(Military Archives)*.

A seemingly young Free State soldier searching a cart in Dublin *(Mercier Archives)*.

A Free State search warrant for the home of Robert Briscoe's mother in ▷ Monkstown, dated 11 July 1922. They were looking for Briscoe himself, who was born in Dublin into a Jewish family of German and Lithuanian origins. During the War of Independence Briscoe was involved in procuring weapons for the IRA in Germany (where he had worked prior to the First World War). He took the anti-Treaty side in the Civil War. Around the time that this warrant was issued, he travelled to London and thence to New York. Briscoe later served as a Fianna Fáil TD and Lord Mayor of Dublin; he was also involved in smuggling Jewish refugees to Palestine in 1939 and 1940 *(Kilmainham Gaol Museum)*.

# DAIL EIREANN
## Defence Department.

---

## SEARCH WARRANT.

As upon information received by me I am satisfied that there is reason to suspect that the premises

situated at _Monkstown and known as "Marino" (BRISCOE)_

are being used for the purpose of _harbouring Mutineers and storing_

_their Arms and Ammunition_

now I _Niall mac Néill_ , Brigadier

hereby authorise you _Lieutenant Thomas_ Rank _Lambert_

to proceed with a Search party to, and to enter ~~in the daytime~~ into the aforesaid premises and there make

search for the _the Mutineers, Arms and Ammunition_ above mentioned,

and to make the necessary seizures, and to bring the same, and the persons in whose possession the same may

be found to me at _Harbour Barracks, Dún Laoghaire —_

Dated this _11th_ . day of _July_ 19 _22_ .

Signed

_Niall mac Néill_ Brigadier

O/C No 2 Brigade 2nd Eastern Div.

Ósglais na n-Éireann

1 1 JULY 1922

HEADQUARTERS No 2 BRIGADE

2nd. Eastern Division

# MOUNTJOY JAIL

To H. ——
Tuesday, 11th July, 1922,
A Chara,
Seventh Year of the Republic.

In reply to yours asking for the truth as to the diet here—

Official Menu.                    What we get.

## BREAKFAST.

| | |
|---|---|
| 1 Pint Tea. | The "Government" has not given us Tea since our arrival. |
| 8 Ozs. **Bread** | Yes. |
| ½ Oz. **Butter**. | We got Butter twice. Margarine on other occasions. |
| 1 Pint Stirabout. | Nobody outside would recognise this as Porridge. We don't know what it is. |
| ½ Pint Milk. | This is served on top of the "Stirabout" and owing to the taste of the latter, we are not sure that it is milk. Perhaps it is. |

## DINNER.

| | |
|---|---|
| 4 Ozs. **Meat**, served with Broth. | Yes. Always stewed and cold. |
| 1lb. **Potatoes**. | Absolutely inedible. Eaten by some to avoid starvation. |
| 4 Ozs. **Cabbage**. | Yes. Always Cold. |
| 4 Ozs. **Bread**. | Yes. |

## FRIDAY DINNER.

| | |
|---|---|
| 4 Ozs. **Bread**. | Yes. |
| 1lb Potatoes. | See above. |
| 1 Pt. Vegetable Soup | Yes. |
| 2 Ozs. Rice. | We have never received rice. |
| 1 Pint Milk. | Yes. |

## SUPPER.

| | |
|---|---|
| 1 Pint Tea or Cocoa | Neither. |
| 8 Ozs. Bread. | Yes. |
| ¾ Ozs. Butter. | See above. |
| ½ Pint Milk. | Occasionally. |

The meat has to be taken in the fingers and torn. The potatoes peeled by hand. We are supplied with a horn spoon

Under the British Government regime food parcels were allowed to prisoners except criminals.

We are often aroused at night by aimless shooting by sentries. The most serious matter perhaps is the unhygenic condition. No man has more than one towel (for toilet and washing-up purposes) and some have none at all. We have succeeded in getting a few sweeping brushes after a long delay. No disinfectants are supplied.

**The "Government" cannot break the Spirit of the men here either by starvation or disease. We defy them.**

Beir Buadh 7 Beannacht
RORY O'CONNOR

◄ Republican propaganda alleging harsh conditions in Mountjoy Prison, dated 'seventh year of the republic'. The surrender of the anti-Treaty garrisons in Dublin ensured that Dublin's prisons were now filled with republican prisoners taken into custody by the Free State *(Dublin City Library and Archive, Birth of the Republic collection).*

The spread of the Civil War outside Dublin saw the new National Army expand enormously. Here, a crowd waits outside a recruiting office on Pearse Street *(National Library of Ireland).*

*Mac... Gift*

## IRISH REPUBLICAN ARMY,
### H. Q. of 2nd Eastern Division,
### Wellington Barracks,
### 27th July, 1922

# MILITARY ORDER.

The Officer commanding 2nd Eastern Division (which includes the County and City of Dublin) hereby warns all Proprietors of Licensed Houses that it is prohibited to supply members of the Irish Army in uniform with intoxicating liquor.

Where a member of the Irish Forces is found under the influence of drink in a licensed premises the licence of such will be immediately cancelled, and a fine imposed.

The closing regulations must also be enforced in future.

Signed (W. M. for)
T. ENNIS,
Commandant-General I.R.A.

A military order banning publicans from serving members of the National Army, presumably in order to maintain discipline. It is striking that Tom Ennis, the Free State officer on whose behalf it was issued, was still signing himself 'IRA'. Likewise, the letterhead says 'Irish Republican Army', despite the fact that Wellington Barracks (now Griffith College) had been taken over by pro-Treaty forces under Ennis in April 1922. Such confusion was probably inevitable given the chaotic circumstances of the establishment of the Free State. *(National Library of Ireland)*.

# HARRY BOLAND SHOT TRYING

## TO ESCAPE

## Black & Tan Method and the old excuse

---

HARRY BOLAND

Lies Wounded at Death's Door

Shot by Free State Raiders in a Hotel in Skerries

HARRY BOLAND was unarmed

He was arrested at 2 o'clock on Monday Morning

Then was shot trying to escape

He was Shot at 2 o'clock and was only taken to

Hospital six hours later.

ONE UNARMED MAN was surrounded by

6 Armed men

The Town was filled with armed Free Staters

Yet Harry Boland unarmed     surprised in Bed

Could not be arrested without being shot

### SHOT TRYING TO ESCAPE

Harry Boland, is Shot down because he Stood

Faithful to his Oath to the Irish Republic

---

Republican propaganda on the death of Harry Boland, who had taken the anti-Treaty side and who was fatally wounded after being shot by Free State forces in a hotel in Skerries in County Dublin on 31 July 1922; he died the following day *(Dublin City Library and Archive, Birth of the Republic collection).*

The funeral of Arthur Griffith leaving City Hall, where his body had lain in state; he had died of a brain haemorrhage on 12 August 1922 *(National Library of Ireland)*.

The remarkable sight of British officers from the remaining garrison attending Griffith's funeral in the Pro-Cathedral *(National Library of Ireland).*

■ Arthur Griffith's coffin is carried out of the Pro-Cathedral. Amongst the pall-bearers is Michael Collins (marked with an 'X'), whose own funeral would take place from the same venue within a fortnight. Like Griffith, he too would be buried in Glasnevin Cemetery *(National Library of Ireland)*.

The body of Michael Collins is carried from St Vincent's Hospital, Dublin. He had been killed in an ambush in County Cork on 22 August 1922 and his body was transported to Dublin by ship for the funeral. Kevin O'Higgins is visible handling the coffin on the far left. *(National Library of Ireland).*

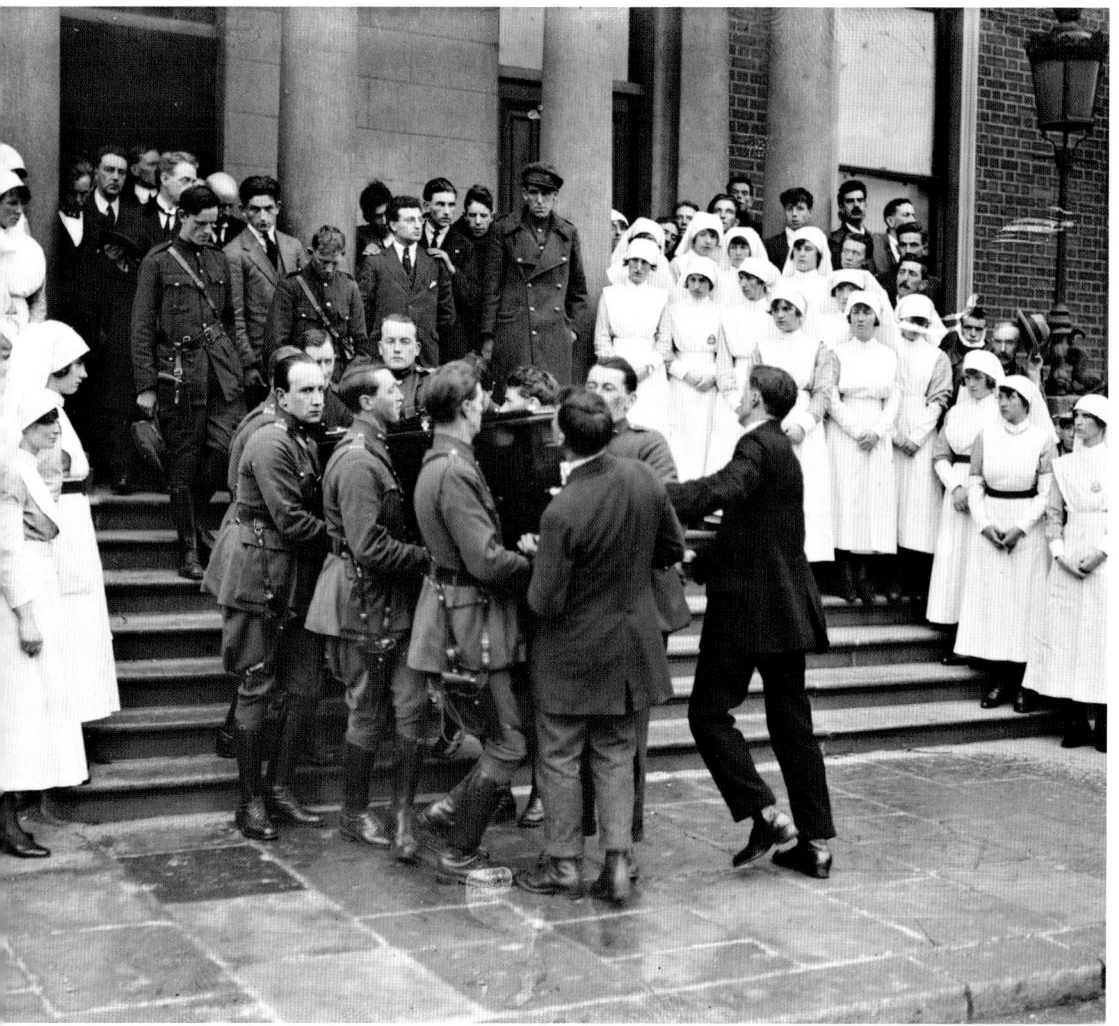

■ Collins's coffin on a gun carriage outside
the Pro-Cathedral, before its departure to
Glasnevin Cemetery *(National Library of
Ireland)*.

Crowds throng O'Connell Street for Collins's
funeral *(National Library of Ireland)*.

■ A mourning car bedecked with wreaths takes part in Collins's funeral procession *(National Library of Ireland).*

Richard Mulcahy (far left, marked with an 'X') leads National Army officers along the wall of Glasnevin Cemetery en route to Collins's graveside. Many of those who made up of the core of the National Army's officer corps consisted of IRA members loyal to Collins, including members of the assassination 'Squad' that he had created *(National Library of Ireland).*

**At the graveside of Michael Collins,**

**General Mulcahy invoked the names of Tom Ashe, Terence MacSwiney, Tomas MacCurtain, and Dick McKee.**

**Hypocrite !**

**He is waging a cowardly war against the nearest and dearest of all these.**

Mulcahy's oration at the graveside of Collins was turned against him by republicans; the reference to Thomas Ashe would have been particularly pointed, as Mulcahy had fought alongside Ashe during the Easter Rising *(Dublin City Library and Archive, Birth of the Republic collection).*

A cartoon depicting the killing of two members of Na Fianna Éireann, presumably by Free State forces. Cole (aged 19) and Colley (aged 21) were senior members of Na Fianna who were apparently involved in reorganising it during the Civil War. They were picked up at Newcomen Bridge on the North Strand, taken out to Whitehall, north of the city, and shot dead. Some of their killers were reported to be wearing National Army uniforms. Such extrajudicial killings by the Free State's security forces became a familiar aspect of the conflict both in Dublin and beyond *(Dublin City Library and Archive, Birth of the Republic collection).*

"Father, Forgive them, for they know not what they do."

Sean Cole, Alf. Colley
Boy Scouts of the FIANNA
Murdered Aug 26. 1922.

■ An armoured car being loaded onto a vessel on the Dublin
quays in the summer of 1922, as the National Army prepared
for seaborne landings in Cork during the Civil War. The vehicle
itself was on the chassis of a Rolls-Royce Silver Ghost. Visible in
the background is a distinctive diving bell, which is still located on
Sir John Rogerson's Quay in Dublin *(National Library of Ireland)*.

Protestors during a postal strike in September 1922. Industrial
action was a fact of life for many workers in Ireland during
the economic upheaval of war and revolution; this dispute
had rumbled on due to cutbacks earlier in the year, and the
eventual strike was the first industrial action taken in the Free
State; the National Army was called in to deal with it and at
one stage strikers at the telephone exchange in Crown Alley
were fired on before an eventual compromise was negotiated
*(Mercier Archives).*

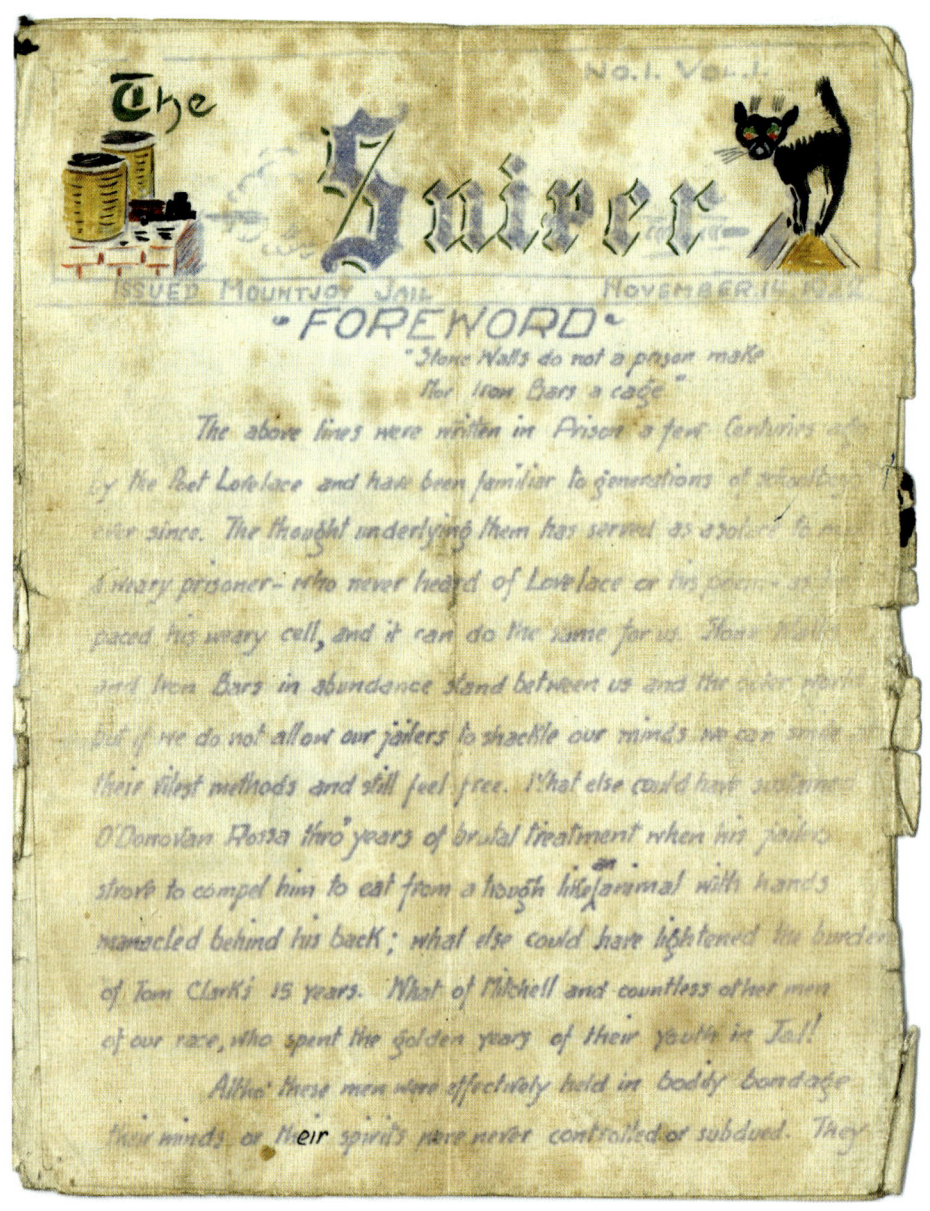

The Sniper

No.1. Vol.1.

ISSUED MOUNTJOY JAIL          NOVEMBER 14 1922

"FOREWORD"

"Stone Walls do not a prison make
Nor Iron Bars a cage"

The above lines were written in Prison a few Centuries ago by the Poet Lovelace and have been familiar to generations of schoolboys ever since. The thought underlying them has served as solace to many a weary prisoner- who never heard of Lovelace or his poems as he paced his weary cell, and it can do the same for us. Stone Walls and Iron Bars in abundance stand between us and the outer world, but if we do not allow our jailers to shackle our minds we can smile at their vilest methods and still feel free. What else could have sustained O'Donovan Rossa thro' years of brutal treatment when his jailers strove to compel him to eat from a trough like an animal with hands manacled behind his back; what else could have lightened the burden of Tom Clark's 15 years. What of Mitchell and countless other men of our race, who spent the golden years of their youth in Jail! Altho' these men were effectively held in bodily bondage their minds or their spirits were never controlled or subdued. They

■ "The Sniper": an unofficial republican newsletter written by prisoners in Mountjoy Prison *(Kilmainham Gaol Museum)*.

```
C O F F I N   S H I P   I N   D U B L I N   B A Y.
))-------------------------------------------------------------------((
                 CONDITION OF PRISONERS ON BOARD.
                 ----------------------------------
```

By order of the Free State Imperial Authorities over 500 prisoners
were taken from Limerick Gaol on Wednesday 30th. ult. and without
food of any kind they were placed on board the S.S. Arvonia.at Limerick
Docks, and arrived in Dublin Bay on Thursday last at 6 p.m. after a
very severe journey.

The men were ordered below the deck by Staff Capt. Frank Bolster
who drove them below at the point of the revolver, saying he would
shoot them before the end of the journey.

The prisoners are now confined in the lower cabin for the past
three days and nights, without sufficient food,air or exercise. The
port holes are closed thereby preventing ventilation of any kind.
The majority of them were on hunger-strike for some days previous
to their leaving Limerick, and most of them are suffering from
swelling of the lower joints caused by insufficient air, exercise,
and want of proper diet, and more especially from overheating of the
place. It is providential that an epidemic has not broken out,
considering that the lavatories ,insufficient in number are without
water except for a few hours per day.

No sleeping accomadation of any kind is provided and consequently
the men are compelled to crowd together on the floor.

Most of the men are in a semi-conscious condition especially the
men whose wounds have not been dressed for the past week; and 50 or
more Fianna Boys whose ages are from 12 years and upwards,are now
lying physically wrecked and in a prostrate condition denied all
medical treatment by Capt. Bolster.

All the men are suffering from thirst as practically no water
is supplied for drinking purposes . The food consists of tea and dry bread
twice daily.

                    SIGNED ON BEHALF OF THE MEN.
                          C.MACKEY . COMDT.

A republican propaganda leaflet on the condition of prisoners. The fact that
this is roughly typed rather than printed is a small indication that such attempts
at publicity were being forced underground as the Free State successfully
prosecuted the Civil War *(Dublin City Library and Archive, Birth of the Republic
collection).*

A memorial card for Rory O'Connor, Liam Mellows, Richard Barrett and Joseph McKelvey, all prominent anti-Treaty republicans who had been imprisoned since the fall of the Four Courts earlier in the year. On 7 December the IRA attacked two members of the new Free State Dáil on Ormond Quay, killing one of them, the veteran Cork IRA leader Sean Hales. This was interpreted by the government, now led by long-standing Sinn Féin politician and 1916 veteran W.T. Cosgrave, as a direct assault on the new Free State, and as a deliberate reprisal these four men were executed without trial by firing squad in Mountjoy Prison the following morning. The ruthlessness of the decision was magnified by the fact that O'Connor had, the previous year, served as the best man at the wedding of Kevin O'Higgins; as Minister for Home Affairs in the Free State government, O'Higgins assented to the execution of his former friend *(Dublin City Library and Archive, Birth of the Republic collection)*.

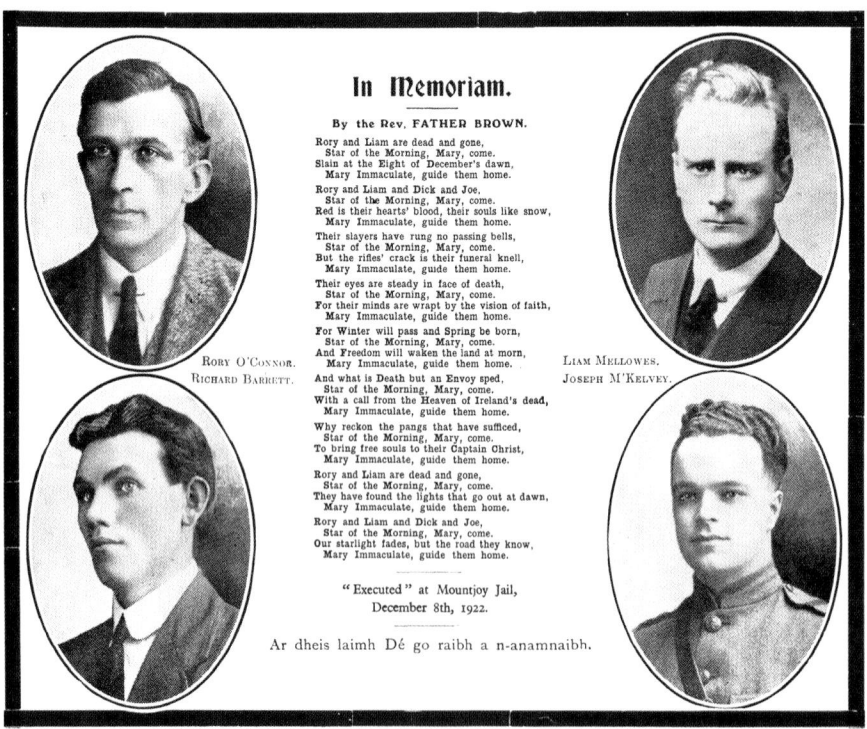

One of Mellows' last notes, written shortly before his execution on 8 December 1922, this time to his friend and fellow republican Eamon Martin. It reads: To my dear comrades in Mountjoy: God bless you, boys, and may He give you fortitude, courage and wisdom to suffer and endure all for Ireland's sake. An Poblacht abú!' *(Dublin City Library and Archive, Birth of the Republic collection)*.

To my dear comrades in Mountjoy:

God bless you, boys, and may He give you fortitude, courage and wisdom to suffer and endure all for Ireland's sake. An Poblacht Abú!

Liam Ó Maoilíosa,

(Liam Mellows.)

Mountjoy Prison,
7.30 A.M.
Dec. 8. 1922

Despatch

Eamon Martin
"C" Wing
Mountjoy Prison

# G O V E R N M E N T      B Y      M U R D E R

On the 6th December 1922 the birth of the so-called Free State is hailed by the sound of guns – English guns in the hands of firing parties for the soldiers of the Irish Republic.

Below we give some details of recent official murders perpetrated by the Little British Ministry in Ireland, details which show the heartlessness and calculated cruelty, never equalled by Russia under the Czar.

The three Dublin boys – Patrick Farrelly, John Murphy and Joseph Spooner ''executed'' on Thursday November 30th all belonged to 'A' Company of the 3rd Battalion, I.R.A., in which they had splendid fighting records during the Black & Tan war. They were arrested on October 30th following an attack in which they took part on Oriel House, the Headquarters of the ''Criminals' Investigation Department'', the criminals being the Murder Gang responsible for the assassination of Harry Boland and the murder of at least six other soldiers of the Irish Republic.

From the time of Joseph Spooner's arrest his people never heard anything from him. He wrote five letters between November 14th and the day of his death. They were all delivered to his people after the 'execution', the news of which was brought to his father by a despatch rider from Portobello Barracks. John Murphy's relatives were treated similarly. It will hardly be believed that on the Monday before his death his father's house was raided by Free State troops who stated to his relatives that he had escaped. They heard nothing further until they got the official notice, between 1 and 2 p.m. on the day of his 'execution'.

In no case were the parents notified that a trial had taken place or was about to take place. And in no case was there any notification given until 5 or 6 hours after the 'execution'. This is probably what Mr. Ernest Blythe meant when he said in the Partition Parliament that they must have 'NO SLOPPY SENTIMENTALITY'.

In his last letter to his father, Patrick Farrelly writes :

'Dear Father, please keep up your heart. I hope all the boys will have a happy New Year. I am quite happy and ready. We will meet in Heaven'.

The following is the last letter written by Joseph Spooner :

                                              J. SPOONER. I.R.A.
                                              BEGGAR'S BUSH.

Dear Father and Mother,

        Goodbye for ever, but please God we shall meet in heaven where we will all rejoice. Tell all my friends and relations to pray for me. Will soon meet Twohig and Fisher as I was the last to see them going. I will die game. Tell MrsEgan she was the last one I saw alive. I asked to see Fr.Morrisey of James' Street Parish and will get him to say a Mass for me on Sunday at 11.30. Bear up, Mother. Tell Martin to pray for me, also Annie and Katie, Mick, May, Mrs.Lynch, Tom and Rosie, the man that worked with my father, Frank and Jane, Billy, Dick, Bridie, also our own children, Katie, Mary, Dick, Annie, Bridie and all the Cauldwells. Tell Mr.O'Connor I asked for him, also all the men at the compound to pray for me and my chums. I die innocent, as God is my judge. I thought I'd live to see Xmas and peace, but please God you will soon have it. Don't take it to heart but try and bear up. I BELONGED TO THE FIANNA FOR FIVE YEARS. Kevin was my O/C and I then went to Skippers' Alley, was under different officers, including Barney Mellowes, Rafferty and James Punch. I JOINED THE IRISH REPUBLICAN ARMY, WAS IN 'A' 3rd FOR TWO YEARS, SO WHEN THE SPLIT CAME I STILL KEPT TO MY COMPANY. So thats my career in the movement. I worked in the Dublin Metal & Galvanising Co.,60 New St.,Dublin. Get all the workers to pray for me.

The last time I say to you to cheer up. Tell my father I was asking for him, tell him to pray for me, also Mrs.L'Estrange and Paddy and the girls we used to be with, Bridie Duncan and Lizzie. So cheer up and pray for me.

                                   You doomed son,
                                        J O S E P H
P.S. Pray for my soul, Mother and Father. LONG LIVE THE REPUBLIC.

◄ 'Government by murder': another unofficial republican publication, this time dwelling on the new policy of executions, which would prove to be perhaps the most bitter legacy of the Civil War *(Dublin City Library and Archive, Birth of the Republic collection).*

Free State soldiers searching a car on a Dublin street, December 1922. ■ While the major fighting in Dublin had ended in July 1922, republican insurgency and Free State counter-insurgency continued in Dublin until the end of the Civil War in April 1923 *(Mercier Archives).*

■ The National Army takes over the Viceregal Lodge in the Phoenix Park, 16 December 1922; to the right, British soldiers can be seen presenting arms. The last remaining British troops were not withdrawn from the Free State until after it officially came into existence on 6 December 1922. The building later served as the official residence of the governor-general, the representative of the British monarch as set out in the Treaty, and eventually became the Irish presidential residence, Áras an Uachtaráin *(National Library of Ireland)*.

Members of the Dublin Command of the National Army at the location of the graves of those IRA members executed and buried in Mountjoy Prison during the War of Independence. In 2001 the so-called 'Forgotten Ten' were reinterred in Glasnevin Cemetery *(Kilmainham Gaol Museum).*

A Lancia armoured car adapted
for use on rail tracks at the
Great Southern and Western
Railway's depot at Inchicore. As
the Civil War intensified outside
Dublin, attacks on railways
became commonplace, and
the National Army created
a dedicated unit to protect
railways; the modified
armoured cars, such as that
in the picture, were used for
this purpose *(National Library
of Ireland)*.

# 1923

Kevin O'Higgins, as Minister for Home Affairs in the Free State government, addresses members of the newly formed Civic Guard from a motorcar in the Phoenix Park depot, 22 February 1923. The Civic Guard (later An Garda Síochána) was the eventual replacement for both the DMP and RIC. O'Higgins himself had been a member of the Irish Volunteers and as TD for Laois had served in the Dáil government; he was blamed for the Free State policy of official executions and was himself assassinated by the IRA in 1927 *(National Library of Ireland).*

A street scene in an unidentified location, with what appears to be a DMP constable in the foreground; Dublin retained its own distinct police force until 1925 when it was incorporated into the Garda Síochána *(National Library of Ireland)*.

The ruins of the Great Northern Line bridge at Portmarnock in north County Dublin, sabotaged by the anti-Treaty IRA in February 1923. Such attacks on infrastructure were commonplace in the later stages of the Civil War *(National Library of Ireland)*.

■ 'Battling Siki', aka Louis M'Barick Fall, in Dublin, with an unidentified companion (left). Siki was a Senegalese heavyweight boxer who fought an Irish contender, Mike McTigue of Clare, in Dublin on St Patrick's Day 1923. The fight was favoured by the authorities, as the international attention it garnered was seen as a good way of asserting to the world that life in the Free State was returning to normal. This was apparently the final twenty-round world title fight ever held; McTigue won on points (possibly a home decision) *(National Library of Ireland).*

IRA paperwork: the Civil War ended in April 1923 with a ceasefire by the IRA, who had essentially been defeated, and an order to dump arms; here the Dublin Brigade attempt to assess what weapons they still had at their disposal *(Military Archives)*.

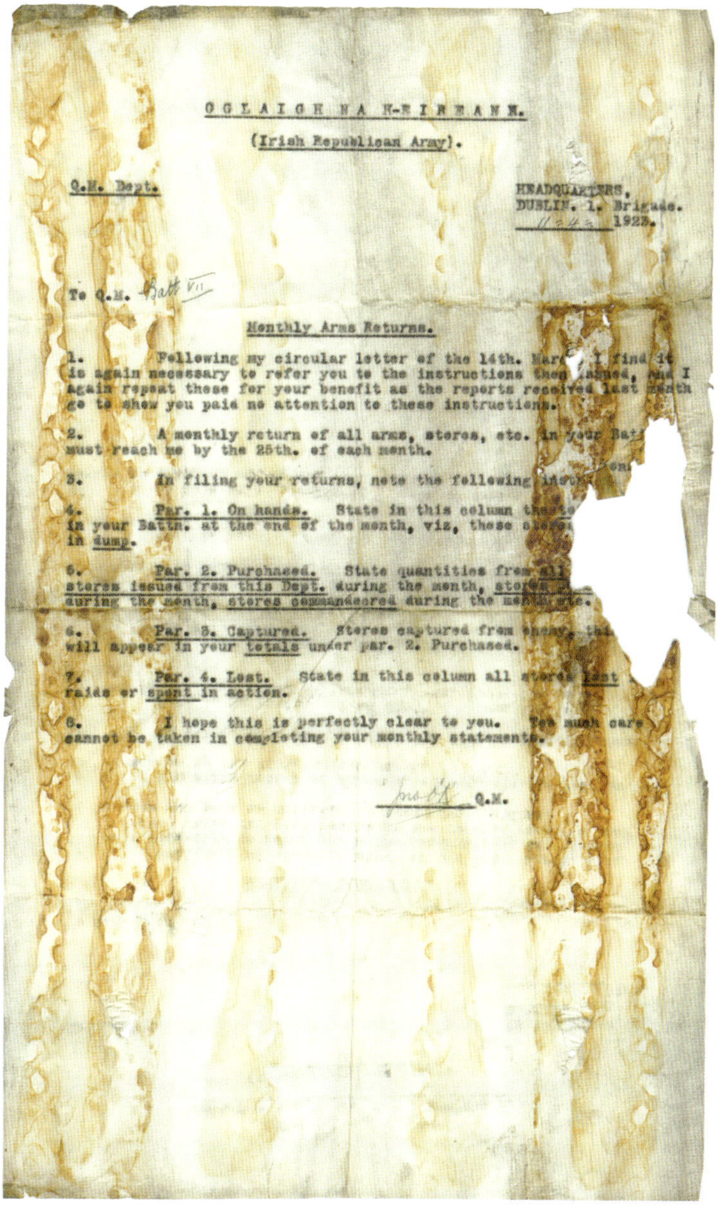

ÓGLAIGH NA H-ÉIREANN.

(Irish Republican Army).

Q.M. Dept.

HEADQUARTERS,
DUBLIN. 1. Brigade.
1923.

To Q.M. Batt VII

Monthly Arms Returns.

1. Following my circular letter of the 14th. March, I find it is again necessary to refer you to the instructions then issued, and I again repeat these for your benefit as the reports received last month go to show you paid no attention to these instructions.

2. A monthly return of all arms, stores, etc. in your Batt. must reach me by the 25th. of each month.

3. In filing your returns, note the following instructions.

4. Par. 1. On hands. State in this column the in your Battn. at the end of the month, viz, those in dump.

5. Par. 2. Purchased. State quantities from all stores issued from this Dept. during the month, stores during the month, stores commandeered during the month etc.

6. Par. 3. Captured. Stores captured from enemy, will appear in your totals under par. 2. Purchased.

7. Par. 4. Lost. State in this column all stores lost raids or spent in action.

8. I hope this is perfectly clear to you. Too much care cannot be taken in completing your monthly statements.

Q.M.

## ABBEY THEATRE
### — DUBLIN. —

Proprietors       THE NATIONAL THEATRE SOCIETY, Ltd

Directors          .    W. B. YEATS, LADY GREGORY

Manager           .     LENNOX ROBINSON

---

Thursday, Friday and Saturday, 12th, 13th and 14th April, at 8.15 p.m.  Matinee Saturday at 2.30.

FIRST PRODUCTION OF

## THE SHADOW OF A GUNMAN

A Tragedy in Two Acts by SEAN O'CASEY.

#### Characters :

| | |
|---|---|
| DONAL DAVOREN | Arthur Shields |
| SEUMAS SHIELDS (a pedlar) | F. J. McCormick |
| TOMMY OWENS | Residents in the Tenement — Michael J. Dolan |
| ADOLPHUS GRIGSON | P. J. Carolan |
| MRS. GRIGSON | May Craig |
| MINNIE POWELL | Gertrude Murphy |
| MR. MULLIGAN (the landlord) | Eric Gorman |
| MR. MAGUIRE | G. V. Lavelle |
| MRS. HENDERSON | residents of an adjoining tenement — Christine Hayden |
| MR. GALLOGHER | Gabriel J. Fallon |
| AN AUXILIARY | Tony Quinn |

SCENE—A room in a tenement in Hilljoy Square, Dublin.

Some hours elapse between the two acts.  The period of the play is May, 1920.

NOTE.—During the second act the sounds customary during a raid by the Auxiliaries are heard.

PRODUCED BY LENNOX ROBINSON.

NOTICE—Owing to numerous Complaints, the Management insist that ladies Sitting in the Stalls shall remove their hats

## SOVEREIGN LOVE
A Comedy in One Act by T. C. MURRAY.

#### Characters :

| | |
|---|---|
| DONALD KEARNEY (a farmer) | Eric Gorman |
| ELLEN | his daughters — Dorothy Lynd |
| KATTY | May Craig |
| MAURICE O'BRIEN (their uncle) | P. J. Carolan |
| MRS. HICKEY (hostess of "The Granuaile") | Eileen O'Kelly |
| CHARLES O'DONNELL (another farmer) | Peter Nolan |
| DAVID (his son) | Tony Quinn |
| TOM DALY (cousin of David) | Barry Fitzgerald |
| ANDY HYDE (a returned Yank) | Michael J. Dolan |

The action takes place in the parlour of "The Granuaile."

---

N.B.—One minute before the beginning of each act a gong is rung and the audience are particularly requested to be in their seats before the curtain rises.

---

The Orchestra, under the direction of Dr. J. F. LARCHET will perform the following selection of music :

| | | |
|---|---|---|
| Overture | "Poet and Peasant" | Suppé |
| Morceaux | 1. "Danse Arabe" 2. "Valse des Fleurs" | Tschaikowsky |
| Excerpt From Symphony No. 6 | 1. Andante 2. Allegretto con grazia | Tschaikowsky |

### NEXT WEEK:

Mr. A. E. FILMER'S COMPANY (Under the auspices of the Dublin Drama League).

Monday, Tuesday, Wednesday and Saturday at 8.15 p.m. Matinee Saturday at 2.30.

MISALLIANCE BY GEORGE BERNARD SHAW Thursday and Friday at 8.15 p.m.

SIX CHARACTERS IN SEARCH OF AN AUTHOR BY LUGI PIRANDELLO

---

■ The programme for the debut run of Sean O'Casey's tragi-comedy *The Shadow of a Gunman* at the Abbey Theatre, April 1923. The play was set in a tenement, and the main protagonist is a struggling poet who is mistaken for an IRA man on the run (a notion he does little to dispel, with disastrous results). The setting was apparently inspired by a tenement on Mountjoy Square in which O'Casey had lived during the War of Independence. Note the reassurance to patrons that the sounds of a raid in Act 2 were part of the performance, rather than reality, an indication of how such upheaval had become part and parcel of everyday life *(Abbey Theatre)*.

A republican meeting amidst the ruins of O'Connell Street, August 1923, with a tricolour clearly visible *(National Library of Ireland).*

■ The end of the Civil War did not bring an end to the pursuit of suspects, as seen by the detention order for Kitty Harpur of Cumann na mBan, signed by Richard Mulcahy *(Kilmainham Gaol Museum)*.

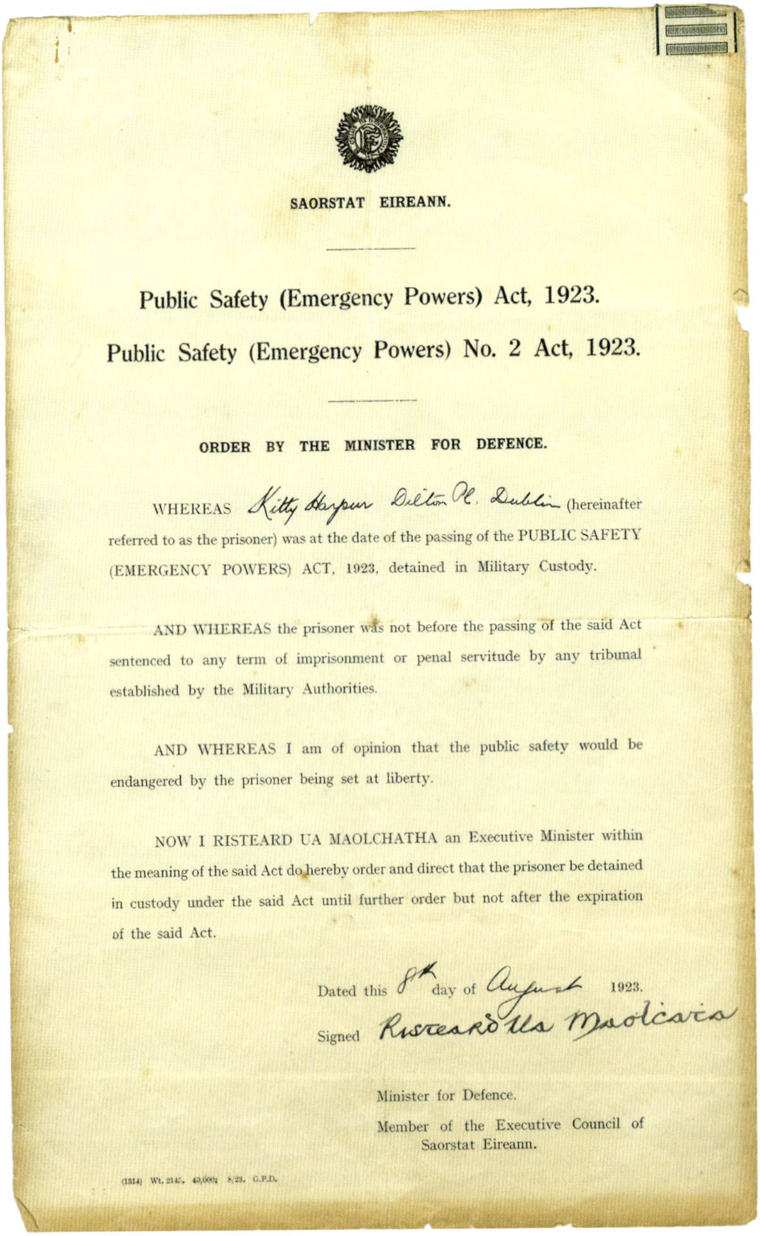

SAORSTAT EIREANN.

Public Safety (Emergency Powers) Act, 1923.

Public Safety (Emergency Powers) No. 2 Act, 1923.

ORDER BY THE MINISTER FOR DEFENCE.

WHEREAS *Kitty Harpur Dilton Pl. Dublin* (hereinafter referred to as the prisoner) was at the date of the passing of the PUBLIC SAFETY (EMERGENCY POWERS) ACT, 1923, detained in Military Custody.

AND WHEREAS the prisoner was not before the passing of the said Act sentenced to any term of imprisonment or penal servitude by any tribunal established by the Military Authorities.

AND WHEREAS I am of opinion that the public safety would be endangered by the prisoner being set at liberty.

NOW I RISTEARD UA MAOLCHATHA an Executive Minister within the meaning of the said Act do hereby order and direct that the prisoner be detained in custody under the said Act until further order but not after the expiration of the said Act.

Dated this *8th* day of *August* 1923.

Signed *Risteárd Ua Maolcáta*

Minister for Defence.
Member of the Executive Council of Saorstat Eireann.

(1314) Wt. 2145, 40,000; 8/23. G.P.D.

The Athlone-born tenor John McCormack – a global star in his lifetime – lays a wreath at the temporary memorial erected to Collins and Griffith at the rear of Leinster House and unveiled on 12 August 1923. Designed by George Atkinson, it was made of wood overlaid with plaster, and was adorned with medallions designed by Albert Power and representing the two dead leaders. The memorial weathered badly and plans to erect a more permanent version never came to pass. It was eventually removed in 1939; in 1950 a granite obelisk was erected in its place *(Library of Congress)*.

# MEN ON HUNGER-STRIKE
## LIST OF DUBLIN PRISONERS

| | | | |
|---|---|---|---|
| GEO. PLUNKETT | 26 Upr. Fitzwilliam Street | PAT O'NEILL | 7 Park Tce., Francis Street |
| MALACHI SWEETMAN | 47 Merrion Square | WM. MALONE | 83 Cork Street, Dublin |
| SEAN RUSSELL | 68 North Strand Road | HENRY CASEY | 22 Eugene Street |
| SEAMUS O'DONOVAN | 13 Grace Park Gardens, Drumcondra | JAS. CASSIDY | 13 Lower Mount Street |
| DAN O'DONOVAN | do.          do. | J. McDONNELL | Victoria Cottage, Stillorgan Road |
| D. L. ROBINSON | Stephen's Green Club | H. ARDIFF | 70 Lower Kilmainham |
| ML. DOYLE | 16 Waterloo Lane | F. BRENNAN | Finglas, Co. Dublin |
| LEO J. HENDERSON | 5 Windsor Villas, Fairveiw | P. EVERS | 28 George's Place, Dublin. |
| DAN O'DONNELL | 30 Glengariffe Parade | L. POWER | 27 Upr. Gloucester Street |
| ERNIE O'MALLEY | | M. TUOHY | 62 Pimlico |
| WM. WYSE | Jamestown Road Finglas | W. CASEY | 4 Weaver Square, Dublin |
| PAT THOMAS | 14 Tubbermore Ave, Dalkey | B. CORCORAN | Blackrock |
| ED. CAMPBELL | Balbriggan | J. PIDGEON | 29 Coombe, Dublin |
| WM. THORNTON | 7 Lower Dominick Street | A. McDONNELL | 20 Up. Mt. Pleasant Av. Rathmines |
| SEAN BURKE | 32 Lr. Gloucester Street | B. EGAN | 15 Lindsay Road, Glasnevin |
| ML. McGANN | 32 Townsend Street | J. McKENNA | Finglas |
| MATT CONNOLLY | King's Ave. Ballybough Rd. | R. LAWLESS | c/o Miss Dowling, 143 North Strand Road |
| CHAS. MURPHY, T.D. | 4 Sydney Terrace, S.C.Rd. | P. WHITE | 7 Clanbrassil Ter., S.C.R. |
| PAT SWEENEY | 16 Cadogan Road, Fairveiw | ROBERT HEGARTY | 10 Charlemont Mall, Portobello |
| ML. PRICE | 15 Killarney Parade, N.C.R. | ARTHUR RING | 11 Ormond Market |
| C. KELLY | Church Street, Skerries | SEAN HEALY | 32 North King Street |
| H. LANG | 15 Botanic Road | JOHN REDMOND | Killininny, Tallaght |
| WM. CREIGHTON | 27 Patrick St. Dunlaoghaire | LEO REED | 53 North Circular Road |
| LOUIS ROBINSON | 56 Blessington Street | PETER O'CONNOR | 40 "A" Road, Fairbrother's Field's, S.C.R. |
| DAN TYNAN | 16 St. Teresa's Place, Glasnevin | FRANK CASEY | 60 Shelbourne Road, Ballsbridge |
| PAT BYRNE | Hardwicke Street | PATRICK MORRISSEY | 7 Gullstan Ter., Rathmines |
| JOHN FARRELL | Portrane Asylum | WM. MEGAN | 1 Meaney Avenue, Dalkey |
| JOE O'TOOLE | 23 Upr. Wellington Street | JAMES ARDIFF | 70a Old Kilmainham |
| A. O'ROURKE | Shankhill, Co. Dublin | FRANK HENDERSON | 75 North Circular Road |
| JAS. FARRELL | do.          do. | J. C. FORDE | 32 Gardiner's Place |
| GEO. KERR | Rathmines | SEAN MacBRIDE | 73 St. Stephen's Green |
| PAT BARRON | do. | ML. CUNNINGHAM | 6 Grangegorman Villas, N.C.R. |
| JAS. MALLIN | Mountbrown, Dublin | GERALD BOLAND, T.D. | Charlemont House, Fairview |
| SEAN McGLYNN | 4 Portobello Harbour | THOMAS McMAHON | 10 Lomond Av., Fairview |
| C. WATERS | 17 Harold's Rd. Manor St., & Waterford | J. McHENRY | 19 North Brunswick St. |
| D. KERRIGAN | 13 Carnew St., N.C.R. | JAMES O'CONNOR | 179 McCaffrey Estate, Mt. Brown |
| LEO FARRELL | 15 Pym Street | P. BRENNAN | 6 Pembroke Ter., Main St., Dundrum |
| JOHN O'CALLAGHAN | 2 Harcourt Place | SEUMAS O'BRIEN | 19 Ely Place |
| MATTIE KELLY | 27 Upper Rutland Street | H. PENDER | 6 Dolphin's Barn Street |
| JOHN CRUISE | 57 Botanic Avenue | | |

## Go m-beannuighidh Dia d'on Poblacht

◀ A list of republican prisoners from Dublin on hunger strike in Dublin in October and November 1923. This hunger strike was undertaken to force the Free State government into releasing its prisoners after the end of the Civil War and lasted from 13 October to 23 November. Two prisoners died but the hunger strike failed in its objective *(National Library of Ireland)*.

## Le Petit Journal

12 Pages                                                    12 Pages

HEBDOMADAIRE        ══ *illustré* ══        PRIX : 0 fr. 30
61, rue Lafayette, Paris                                28 Octobre 1923

**A l'Exemple du Maire de Cork**

Quatre cent vingt-quatre Irlandais, enfermés dans la prison de Montjoie, à Dublin, s'étant vus refuser leur mise en liberté, ont décidé la grève de la faim. En vain, les gardiens s'efforcent-ils de les faire céder en leur présentant une nourriture abondante. Depuis le 14 octobre, les prisonniers s'entêtent dans leur farouche résolution.

A French newspaper carries a report on the hunger strike in Dublin in its front cover, making a link to Terence MacSwiney, the Lord Mayor of Cork who had died on hunger strike in 1921 *(National Library of Ireland)*.

# Facts that speak for themselves

A young man called Armstrong was found shot in his garage. The Coroner's verdict was "shot by some person unknown." He was an ardent supporter of the Union Jack: so over 150 Republicans, belonging to all classes of society and varying occupations, have been arrested, without warrant, and imprisoned without trial, on suspicion, and hundreds of Republican homes have been raided.

## CONTRAST WITH THE FOLLOWING :—

1. Commandant Sean Cole
2. Vice-Brigadier Alfred Colley } Arrested on Newcomen Bridge, 26th August, 1922. Dead bodies found Yellow Lane, Drumcondra.

3. Captain B. Daly—Arrested 26th August. Taken in a Ford Car. Dead body found St. Doulough's, Malahide Road.

4. M. Neville (grocer's assistant, Mooney's, Eden Quay)—Arrested at his work, 27th September, 1922. Dead body found at Killester.

5. Holahan
6. Hughes } (Young boys).—Arrested while posting up Republican literature, October, 1922. Dead bodies found at Clondalkin.
7. Rodgers

8. Thomas O'Leary—Arrested Upper Rathmines, 1922. Dead body found near Tranquilla Convent.

9. Section-Commander Frank Lawlor—Arrested at his lodgings, 29th December, 1922. Dead body found at Milltown.

10. Stephens (a Volunteer from Ulster)—Arrested in Dublin in 1922. Dead body found at 3rd Lock, Inchicore.

11. Noel Lemass—Arrested outside Wicklow Hotel, 1923. Dead body found on the mountains near Glencree.

12. Quarter-Master Chris. Breslin
13. T. Kiernan } Arrested in Wexford Street, 14 April, 1923. Dead bodies found at Cabra.

14. Martin Hogan (foreman) Arrested in Dorset Street, 21st April, 1923. Dead body found, Grace Park Road, Drumcondra.

15. Robert Bonfield (student)—Arrested in St. Stephen's Green on Holy Thursday, 1923. Dead body found on Good Friday, at Clondalkin.

16. Leo Murray
17. Rodney Murphy } (of Grange)—Arrested together, 1923. Dead bodies found at Stillorgan.

18. Captain Harry MacEntee (carpenter)—Arrested as he left his work, August, 1923. Dead body found Poppintree Lane, Ballymun.

No one has been brought to justice for any of these hideous murders. The murdered men were Republicans and opponents of Mr. Cosgrave's ministry and of the Union Jack

THE FODHLA PRINTING CO., LTD., DUBLIN.

## WILL YOU BE THERE ?

TO PAY HOMAGE TO THE MEMORY
OF

### Liam, Rory, Dick and Joe

**1st Anniversary Commemoration Concert**

# THEATRE ROYAL

*Sunday, December 9, 1923*

AT 8 P.M., SHARP.

## St. James's Band

Will perform the following :—
"The Reminiscences of Grieg"
"The Dramatic Symphony in
B Minor." Schubert.

**RAFFLE FOR SOUVENIRS OF MARTYRED MEN**
entitle Programme Holders to participate.

Seats can be Booked at MAIRE NI RAGHAILLAIGH'S,
87 Upper Dorset Street. 'Phone 184.

## The Connolly Pipers' Band

PRICES :—Dress Circle, 3/-; Parterre, 2/-; Upper
Circle, 1/6; Gallery, 1/-; Boxes £1, 30/-,
£2; Box Seats. 5/- each.

A flyer for a commemoration of the executed anti-Treaty republicans ■ Mellows, O'Connor, Barrett and McKelvey, on the first anniversary of their deaths. As was the case after 1916, the deaths of republicans would be remembered after the Civil War to foster support for a cause that seemed to be defeated. As far as republicans were concerned, some, if not all, had lived to fight another day *(Dublin City Library and Archive, Birth of the Republic collection).*

■ *Flowerland*: a reminder of normality, in the form of a charitable performance at the Abbey Theatre to raise money for impoverished children in Dublin. The city's chronic social problems were not tackled in any meaningful way during the upheavals of the revolution *(National Library of Ireland)*.

# SELECT BIBLIOGRAPHY

Connell, Joseph E.A., *Michael Collins' Dublin, 1916–22* (Dublin, 2017)

Crowley, John, Donal Ó Drisceoil and Mike Murphy (eds), John Borgonovo (associate ed.), *Atlas of the Irish Revolution* (Cork, 2017).

*Dictionary of Irish Biography* (7 vols, Cambridge, 2009).

Dorney, John, *The Civil War in Dublin: The Fight for the Irish Capital, 1922–24* (Dublin, 2017).

Fallon, Las, *Dublin Fire Brigade and the Irish Revolution* (Dublin, 2012).

Gibney, John, and Donal Fallon, *Revolutionary Dublin: A Walking Guide, 1912–23* (Cork, 2018).

Gillis, Liz, *The Fall of Dublin* (Cork, 2011).

Gillis, Liz, *Revolution in Dublin: A Photographic History, 1913–1923* (Cork, 2013)

Irish, Tomás, *Trinity in War and Revolution, 1912–23* (Dublin, 2015)

Ó Conchubair, Brian (ed.), *Dublin's Fighting Story, 1916–21: Told By The Men Who Made It* (2nd ed. Cork, 2009)

Ó Ruairc, Padraig Óg, *Revolution: A Photographic History of Revolutionary Ireland, 1913–23* (Cork, 2011)

Price, Dominic, *We Bled Together: Michael Collins, the Squad, and the Dublin Brigade* (Cork, 2017)

Sheehan, William, *Fighting for Dublin: The British Battle for Dublin, 1919–21* (Cork, 2007).

Yeates, Padraig, *A City in Turmoil: Dublin, 1919–21* (Dublin, 2013)

Yeates, Padraig, *A City in Civil War: Dublin, 1921–23* (Dublin, 2015)

Yeates, Padraig, *Rioters, Looters, Lady Patrols & Mutineers: Some Reflections On Lesser Visited Aspects of the Irish Revolution in Dublin* (Dublin, 2017)

Walsh, Maurice, *Bitter Freedom: Ireland in a Revolutionary World* (London, 2015)

Wren, Jimmy, *The GPO Garrison Easter Week 1916* (Dublin, 2015)

# INDEX

Pearse Station see Westland Row Station
Pearse Street see Great Brunswick Street
*Petit Journal, Le*, 217
Phoenix Park, 19, 48, 202
*Plough and the Stars, The* (O'Casey), 7
Plunkett, George, 116, 137
Plunkett, Joseph Mary, 137
Portmarnock, 209
postal strikes, 195
Power, Albert, 215
Pro-Cathedral, 48, 185–6, 188
Provisional Government, 130, 134–6, 150–51
Public Record Office, 155, 157

Red Cross, 173
Restoration of Order in Ireland Act, 84
Royal Army Medical Corps, 104
Royal Barracks (now Collins Barracks), 65
Royal Dublin Fusiliers, 34
Royal Exchange Hotel, 71
Royal Irish Constabulary (RIC), 4, 51, 66, 77, 85,
    207
Rummings, Victor B., 20–22
Russian Revolution, 25

Sackville Street (now O'Connell Street), 86–7,
    100, 118, 137, 141, 147, 154, 158, 161–71,
    174, 189–90, 213
St Vincent's Hospital, 187
Savage, Martin, 48–9
*Shadow of a Gunman* (O'Casey), 212
Shelbourne Hotel, 136
Sinn Féin, 1, 11, 15, 29–33, 34, 37, 46, 50, 58–9,
    93, 111, 130, 144
slums, 70
'Sniper, The', 196
Solemn League and Covenant, 13
Soloheadbeg ambush, 34, 72
South Dublin Union, 42, 141, 176
Spanish Flu pandemic, 1, 24, 28
'Squad', the, 191
Stephens, James, 5

'TNT Mick', 62
Traynor, Oscar, 160
Treacy, Sean, 72
Trinity College Dublin, 64
truce, 112–16, 150
'Trucileers', 150

University College Dublin, 68

Viceregal Lodge (now Áras an Uachtaráin), 19,
    51, 202

Walsh, William, 46–7
War of Independence, 1, 34, 48–109, 178, 203
Wellington Barracks, 182
Westland Row Station (now Pearse Station), 85
Westmoreland Street, 138
Whelan, Thomas, 92–3
Wilson, Sir Henry, 151

FIRST PUBLISHED IN 2018 BY
The Collins Press
West Link Park
Doughcloyne
Wilton
Cork
T12 N5EF
Ireland

A CIP record for this book is available from the British Library.

Hardback ISBN: 978-1-84889-355-9

Design and typesetting by Gigantic Media
Typeset in Bebas Neue & OpenSans
Printed in Poland by Białostockie Zakłady Graficzne SA

Supported by Glasnevin Trust

FOUNDED IN 1828
GLASNEVIN TRUST
DARDISTOWN    GLASNEVIN    GOLDENBRIDGE
NEWLANDS CROSS    PALMERSTOWN

Cover photographs
Front: A propaganda image of the IRA patrolling Grafton Street,
June 1922 (Mercier Archives).
Back: An Easter Rising commemoration, April 1922 (Mercier Archives).

Photograph on pp i–iii: The burning shell of the 'Block' seized
by the anti-Treaty forces in 1922.